A JOURNEY ACROSS NORTH AMERICA

BY DANIEL COOPER

EDITED BY
ANNIE MCDONALD AND LYNSEY MEANS

This book is dedicated to my dear friends Preston and Josh.

Their courageous stories will live on in the hearts of so many. This one's for you, Preston Baehr and Josh "The Gentle Giant" Blankenship. I love you both dearly and I can't wait to see you in Heaven.

-Contents-

- INTRODUCTION -

I t was one of those things I had only seen in the movies or read about in the newspapers. The thought of it ever happening to somebody close to me never really crossed my mind. I definitely never expected it to happen to me. But it did. Suddenly, I found myself standing in a sea of emotions, being choked by the waters of my own confusion. I remember hearing those words and how they made me feel like I was drowning. I remember feeling overwhelmed. I remember feeling uncertainty. I remember feeling an eerie sense of nothingness.

There was this internal, emotional struggle; a chaotic game of tug-of-war taking place inside of me. On one side of the rope stood an infinite number of emotions and uncertainties, and on the other side was the monster known as CANCER.

Sometimes I think it is beneficial to experience things that leave us in these positions. I think that it can be healthy for us to be left in a place where we honestly have no idea what we are going to say or do. I think that life has a way of placing us in these positions (dare I call them crossroads) to prepare us for something bigger than we could ever imagine.

When I met the monster known as cancer, I was already in the midst of a four-year journey spent wandering down a road of self-pity. On this journey, I spent many of my days and most of my nights in bars. I drank nearly every night. I would find any reason to have a drink. I made excuses for my drinking. I drank with strangers. I drank with friends. I even remember going to work a few times still drunk from the previous night. I didn't realize it at the time, but I was actually learning how destructive the choices we make in life can actually be.

Miles down the road that made up this journey, things became bumpy. I was left with two options: I could continue to travel down the same road, or veer onto a completely different one. I decided then and there to veer. The new road seemed scary and appeared to be paved with doubt, but there was no turning back; I had officially headed down the road of uncertainty.

As the doctor stood there with me in that room, giving me the information that I never wanted to hear, my life changed. Not only did I decide to take this new road, but I also decided to change my priorities. It was in this moment that I found myself pulled toward something that felt so foreign and so distant, yet so familiar and so close. It was in that moment that I decided to return to my faith.

Now I feel as though I should pause here and ask that you not stop reading just because I dropped the f-bomb. I am well aware that the word "faith" can carry a certain stench with it. I understand the stigma that may arise with the use of such a word. You may be thinking right now, "Oh no, this Bible-thumper is going to attempt to use this self-help book to convert me from my pagan ways." Before we go any further, I want you to know this: *Coffee with Cooper* is *not* a self-help book. It is also not a book full of Christian catchphrases with a hidden agenda to convert the masses. I will however point out that, yes, I am a Christian and at times you may perceive that in my writing style; but, I would like to encourage you to continue reading without feeling like you are being set up to be my "project." My simple desire while writing *Coffee with Cooper* is for you to experience some of what I did on this life-changing journey. It is also my hope that you relate to some of what you read, and that you potentially find encouragement through the experiences I encountered on this journey and my attempt to remain positive in the midst of cancer.

When I first heard the word "cancer," my world stopped. I remember it like it was yesterday. The doctor walked in with her chart in hand. She looked at me and immediately began to give me the news. She began by saying that the first two of three tumors they had tested contained no cancer.

I could tell by the way she used the phrase "the first two" that the third probably carried with it some bad news. And then she said it: "The third tumor tested positive for a cancer known as peripheral nerve sheath sarcoma."

A million thoughts began to run through my mind as I tried to focus on what the doctor had just informed me, and what she was telling me would happen next. She went on and on about some of the possible options that I would need to consider. She told me that I would need to see a number of other doctors over the next couple of weeks in order to make the best possible choices. I did everything I could to stay with her in that moment, but I could feel myself getting lost. It was as though I was being sucked into an alternate reality. Physically I was there, but emotionally and mentally I was somewhere completely different.

As I left the room where my life was changed forever, I walked up to the receptionist's desk where I was handed a piece of paper. The paper, which felt as though it was nearly a mile long, was full of the names of different doctors whom I would be seeing for what I could only assume would be an eternity. The receptionist began to explain the list that he had just handed me. In that moment it felt as though my life was officially over. I had a horde of doctors to see, I had no insurance, and…I had cancer. What was I going to do? How was I going to tell my mom? What does this all really mean? Am I a dead man walking? The floodgates had officially opened and the questions continued pouring through my mind. The receptionist continued guiding me through what was to come, but I wasn't really listening and it really didn't matter. I had the list and it was clear that there would be a lot of doctors and a lot of appointments. In the moment, nothing he had to say was relevant to me. The bomb had already been dropped. I knew that I had cancer.

When my friend arrived to pick me up at the hospital, I was certain he could tell by the look in my eyes that the prognosis was not good. In those situations, people always want to have the perfect thing to say. When they hear you say the words "I have cancer" they get that glazed look in their eyes. This is usually followed by a lump in their throat which they struggle to swallow. When that lump fails to dissipate, they sigh. No matter how hard they try to hold it in, it is almost always a long, airy, painful sigh, followed by…"the apology." "I am so sorry. I am so sorry. I wish I could think of something else to say, but…I don't know what else to say. I am just so sorry."

People tend to become extremely sympathetic when they learn you are fighting cancer, especially when the odds are not in your favor. I had a lot of people to share my news with, so I became very familiar with a standard reaction and response. Looking back, I never expected anyone to have the perfect words to say in response to my diagnosis. Months after my diagnosis, I still don't expect that.

I immediately developed an understanding that no one, not even one with the formation of the most eloquent statement of sympathy, could repair the damage to my body. This attitude that formed from that understanding seemed to be one that eased the minds of the recipients of my news. Many were shocked by my ability to boldly stare into the face of my attacker and at times to even laugh at the monster known as cancer. I made it clear to those around me that I wasn't going to allow cancer to define me. It was this very mindset that helped develop a strange level of peace within the very people who moments before were attempting to lavish me with sympathetic words.

I took notice of this unusual reaction of those around me and further explored this idea of hope and strength in the midst of my battle with cancer. I felt a power in my desire to be courageous as I continued to share my story with my family, friends, and even complete strangers. Little did I know that these encounters were all a part of something bigger that was making its way to the surface.

After being diagnosed, I had to make a complicated choice that forced me to face some rather difficult possibilities. I was told I would need to decide if I wanted to follow through with treatment or not. There was a great possibility that I would not make it through all of my treatments and that the monster would probably win. I was also told that if I didn't consider treatment I may deal with some equally difficult circumstances. It was a gamble either way. A cloud of fear and uncertainty immediately formed, and I began to dwell on the thought, *What do I do now?*

In spite of my worst fears, I made it through the seven weeks and thirty-five radiation treatments, with only a few side effects. It was then that I gained a deeper sense of hope. That hope not only affected me, but the others with whom I had shared my journey. That got me to thinking, *Now what?*

I began processing all of the moments in which I had already shared my story with others. I realized how often I watched my story of hope inspire those who received it. I began to feel passionate and driven about not only sharing my story, but about meeting others and hearing their story, too.

On January 6, 2014, the idea of Coffee with Cooper could no longer be contained. As the idea surfaced and as the passion behind it began to intensify, I experienced a sense of purpose that I hadn't in some time. As I continued to process what Coffee with Cooper would be and could become, I no longer felt like I was drowning. Now, I felt like I was swimming in a sea of excitement.

Coffee with Cooper was a journey. It was a journey in which I ventured across good old North America! On this journey, I visited coffeehouses in thirty-three different cities and I invested time into the people that I met. In each city and at each coffeehouse, I searched for opportunities to spark up conversations, share my story of hope in the midst of cancer, and hear the stories of others.

The book you are about to read is a collection of thoughts, stories, and experiences that I encountered while on my journey. It is my hope that you will find encouragement through the encounters and stories experienced along the journey that made up Coffee with Cooper. I want to thank you for taking the time to read this book. I believe that we all have the ability to use our own life experiences as a platform. I encourage you to examine your own life and consider using your personal experiences as an instrument to create a beautiful melody. I want to thank you for being a part of *this* story. Thank you for being part of *my* story.

Whether you know me personally or happened to pick up my book through some random course of events, *you* are now a part of the journey, too.

With much love,

Cooper

-THE DRUNK GUY-

I love what you are doing, man. I wish…I wish that I could just get into a car, not know where I was going or what I was going to do, and…do what you are doing, man. I love it!"

With alcohol on his breath, his speech slurred, and a zealous look in his eyes, my friend and host for my week in St. Louis stood outside of his bedroom and confessed his feelings about my adventure. I smiled as he shared his thoughts with me. I smiled, not because I condoned his condition, but because of how positively redundant he was becoming. I smiled because I knew he probably wouldn't remember telling me any of this the next morning.

To be honest, that thought didn't offend me. As I mentioned, prior to my diagnosis I had become very familiar with the influence that alcohol could have on your life. Daily I would use the bottle as a way of dealing with a past that haunted me. Its numbing effects would get me through many nights, but the reality that was the root of my problems would always return to my doorstep the very next morning.

"Coop, you are an artist. Do not let anything discourage you from that."

It was his desire that I allow nothing to hinder me from diligently pursuing the path that had been set for me. He informed me that there would be many obstacles and emotions along the way. He assured me there would be people and things designed to hold me back from doing what I felt so passionate about. My intoxicated friend didn't want me to allow any of these things to distract me from my calling or wane me from my passion. My friend desired that I allow nothing to stop me from what I had set out to do. As he so simply put it, I was going to change the world.

Despite the fact that his blood alcohol content was probably higher than appropriate, I listened as he spoke from the depths of his soul. His head was foggy, but his heart was sincere. And though they were slightly glazed, I could see honesty in his eyes.

I never expected to receive such applicable advice that night from my friend, but I did, and his advice just continued to flow...

"Cancer or noncancer! You started this, you finish it! You cannot give up! Do not give up! Man, some of us are born to be writers, some of us are born to be painters, some of us are born to be musicians. We are all artists in our own special way. *You* were born to do this, and you cannot allow anything to stop you from that. *Not even* you.

"People will say things, things will do things, life will throw curveballs, but you cannot give up. Not many people have the opportunity to do what you are doing, so don't take it for granted. Don't let anything stop you from doing this!"

Then, as suddenly and randomly as this conversation arose, it was over and my friend went to bed. The words he shared with me that night probably should have only taken fifteen to twenty minutes to speak, but the conversation lasted for over an hour. The intensity and passion with which he spoke elongated the conversation. The alcohol obviously slowed things down a bit, too.

I would later discover that this conversation I had with my inebriated friend would became one of the strongest sources of motivation I would carry throughout the course of my journey.

Just as he "warned" me, I faced obstacles that momentarily attempted to distract and deter me from my journey. There were moments where it appeared as though what I was doing was a waste of time. I almost gave up. Almost. But, in many of those moments, I would remember the night I had a conversation with a drunk friend.

"Very few people will have an opportunity to do what you are doing. You were born to do this. Do not let anything stop you from doing this. Not even you. When all the odds are against you, and when it feels the easiest to just cave, don't. You were born to do this!"

-THE SANDWICH-

When I met her, I was in the very beginning stages of my journey. I was in an area close to downtown St. Louis when she walked into the coffeehouse I was sitting in. I had been doing "my thing" for about two days. My brain was buzzing. My emotions were chaotic. Already, within the first two days of starting Coffee with Cooper, I was finding reasons to doubt my ability to accomplish the goal I had set out for. I was already questioning whether or not I had what it took to follow through with the journey. (I realize how pathetic this self-inflicted doubt sounds, but, it's the truth.)

Before CWC started, I created *the* perfect world in my head. This world was one that obviously contained my big journey. In this world, I would enter coffeehouses and within moments of being there, I would find myself surrounded by crowds of people who wanted to know my story. I would then find myself immersed in many intense, deep, life-changing conversations with these people. There, in my head, I was the king of these coffeehouses. And...since this was Coffee with Cooper, every one of these encounters obviously had to take place in a coffee shop! No exceptions.

In this world I had prematurely created, I was changing lives. Through the conversations I was having, I was impacting people in such a meaningful way that they were forever changed. I was a story-telling coffeehouse whisperer. I brought something to the (coffee) table that no other person had or could. I was the element of surprise that shifted the ordinary life into meaningful living. Basically, I was a white, male Oprah of coffeehouses. This was my future and I would not be stopped. Of course, this was all in my head.

Back to reality.

Two days into my big journey, I began to wonder if I really had what it took to accomplish my goal. I began to doubt my ability as a writer, as a conversationalist, and even as a coffeehouse visitor! In the first forty-eight hours of observation, nothing magical had occurred. And as a result, I started to convince myself that my efforts would likely continue to be pointless.

As I sat in this shop, mentally dancing at my own pity party, all I could think about was that, if the rest of my journey was going to be like this, it was going to be a long nine months of nothing but people-watching and coffee-drinking. Don't get me wrong, drinking coffee in forty different cities could never be a bad thing. And I am quite certain that people-watching in that many cities would make for some very interesting stories; but *that was not how I planned for it to be!* In my first two days, I found that I was only having generic, surface-level conversations with the people I met. And "the people" were mostly the baristas who made my coffee. I was beginning to feel bored and disconnected. I started to feel like maybe I should just call it quits.

What? But why? After two days? Why was I even thinking this way?

I took a deep breath, exhaled all my insecurity, and pulled myself together.

If Coffee with Cooper was going to be a success, I knew I was going to have to change my attitude. I knew I was going to need to allow the journey to happen however it happened. I knew I would have to recall the advice my drunk friend had given me. I knew I would need to let things flow in their own natural, organic way, regardless of the depth or lack of conversations that took place. And with that mental epiphany, I put on my big boy pants, kept drinking my Americano, and decided to continue on my path.

As I sat there in this St. Louis coffee shop, wrestling with my own thoughts and emotions, I realized there was a gap in my "being" that my Americano just wasn't filling. It was lunchtime, and I was hungry. I called my friend who was hosting me for the week and expressed my boredom and lack of progress. I asked if we could meet up and get some lunch, mentioning that it would need to be somewhere cheap. I had to eat cheap. Over the next nine months I would be living on $850 a month.

(No kidding. My budget for this trip was super tight! I found that most of my money was consumed by gas, coffee, and ninety-nine cent tacos.)

I was preparing to leave for my lunch rendezvous when I was approached by a woman. She smiled sweetly, and I said, "Hello, how are you?" She answered, and asked if anyone was using the couch next to me. I informed her that it was available and that it would not bother me the slightest bit if she and her boyfriend sat by me. We began to exchange small talk, and I listened cheerfully as she told me a little bit about herself. As we continued to talk, I was thankful for the opportunity to meet such a kind person, but I soon found myself thinking about my friend and our lunch date. I was so hungry.

My new friend continued to talk about her life. She told me about her daughter, her job, and the fact that she loved coffeehouses. She asked me if I frequented the shop in which we were currently sitting. I told her that it was actually my first time visiting and I shared with her my purpose for being there. She was hooked! She asked me all sorts of questions: Where have you been? Where will you go? Are you blogging? How are you getting from city to city? Etc. etc. etc. She was so into the idea of Coffee with Cooper and she wanted to know all she could. I did my best to answer her questions in an informative and meaningful way. With each answer, she had another question. With each question, I continued to think of how hungry I was.

At the end of one of my answers, she looked up at me and said, "Can I buy you a coffee?"

(I feel it is very safe to say that by the end of this journey I had rightfully earned the title "professional freeloader." It was difficult for me in the beginning, because I truly desired to be as self-sufficient as possible, but I soon learned and accepted that there would be many times where I would be offered things like coffee, food, money, etc., by people that I met *and* that in those moments I had to learn to suck up my pride and kindly take people up on their genuine offers.)

As it turned out, I was at my second coffeehouse of the day and I was already working on my sixth or seventh cup of coffee. I was more than convinced that my blood-to-coffee ratio was probably a little off balance. I informed her that having more coffee just then might not be the best idea for me, but I was very thankful she would even offer. It became very clear, very fast, that "no" was not an acceptable answer. She was determined to get me something.

It seemed as though, in response to her being impressed with my story, she felt a need to leave some sort of impression on me. I can say with confidence that she had already left an impression on me. Not just any impression, but a lasting one. I knew the time I spent with her would stick with me through the entirety of this journey and possibly for life. With her, I had the first official, *real* Coffee with Cooper conversation. She was the first of what I found to be a long line of new friends with whom I shared my story and meaningful conversations. She left more than an impression; she got the ball rolling.

Since coffee was not in the forecast for me, she went to the next best thing: food. She asked if she could buy me a sandwich. I actually found myself starting to say that I was getting ready to leave to have lunch with my friend, until I realized how utterly stupid that would have been. Here was a moment where I was finally sharing my story with a stranger, and I was about to pass up continuing our conversation at the expense of a ninety-nine cent taco?

After mentally smacking myself in the face, I called my friend and explained that I would not be meeting up with him, but I would see him later.

I then took my new friend up on her offer and we headed next door for "The Sandwich." In our earlier conversations she had gone on about how wonderful this shop was. I soon discovered just how right she was. "The Sandwich" was a fresh, hot, authentic Italian sandwich. It was the size of a football. It was made with the most tender beef, covered in the perfect amount of melted provolone cheese, and topped with Italian spices and olive oil. It. Was. Wonderful. It was the mothership of all sandwiches. It was way better than any ninety-nine cent taco.

After she paid for my sandwich we headed back over to the coffee shop. We continued chatting, or...I tried to, but most of the time my mouth was so full of sandwich that I found it nearly impossible to speak without revealing all that was in my mouth.

"Don't talk, just eat," she would say as she continued chatting to me.

A couple of times I felt bad because I was unable to answer her questions right away, she would remind me, "Don't talk, just eat."

Quite some time passed while we chatted, and soon it was time for her to leave. She told me how wonderful she thought my planned journey was, and she encouraged me to continue along my way. She informed me that she would tell her daughter and her friends to join the page I had set up to allow others to follow me on my journey.

And with that, she walked out of my life just as quickly as she had walked in.

I cannot help but smile when I think about the perfect timing with which one kind stranger opened the door of a coffee shop. In the moments previous to her arrival, I was ready to give up. If she hadn't walked in that day, I may have abandoned my journey altogether. If I had met her before my doubts arose, I could have skipped the discouragement altogether. But if that had happened, would my short time with her have impacted me to the same extent?

Maybe Coffee with Cooper was not supposed to happen the way that I thought it was. Maybe life is not supposed to happen in the way that we think it should. How different would life be if we just let go of our desires? I am not against having dreams or goals, but when we stick to them so adamantly, leaving no room for natural experiences, are we selling ourselves short? Are we choosing the ninety-nine cent taco over the football-sized Italian sandwich?

-THE TATTOO PARLOR-

I t's sad to admit that we live in a world where we stereotype. As much as we may profess that we personally do not stereotype others, I think it is safe to say that we all do.

The first morning I woke up in St. Louis, I didn't even notice the issue right away. I went about my morning, not doing much of anything (I am, in fact, not much of a morning person). I drank some coffee, collected my thoughts, and prepared for another day that would make up Coffee with Cooper.

As I went about my morning, something felt off. Something in my current state of existence just didn't feel right. It almost felt as though the balance of the universe was slightly askew. Weird, I know! And then...I realized what it was.

I was missing a ball!

Really! I was.

When I became aware of this anomaly of self, I was overwhelmed with a feeling of insecurity. I thought back to the night before, and replayed the events that had made up my evening. I searched for any reason that this could be happening to me.

I knew that when I had fallen asleep everything had been there, but...now? It was as if "it" had vanished into thin air.

Do balls even do that? Vanish?!

I looked frantically for my ball. I looked everywhere that I could think to look, but it was nowhere to be found. My feeling of self-worth was quickly declining. The last thing I wanted to deal with on this journey was the absence of a ball. It was one of the many things I had hoped to use to meet people. My ball was one of the things I was certain would help me connect with some of the people I would come in contact with along the way.

I was torn, I was conflicted, and I had no idea what I was going to do. Until it hit me.

I had an idea. I would call one of the only people that I knew could help me in this situation. I would call the one person who could tell me what to do. I would call...the girl who pierced my nose and I would ask her what I should do about the missing piece in my piercing. Aka, the ball that held in my piercing. (What did you think I was talking about!?)

You see, what had happened was that when I had gone to sleep the night before, my nose piercing was nice and snug in its place. When I woke up the next morning, the ball that held in the stud in my nose had come loose and fallen off. I have no idea where it went because I never found it. I also have no idea how it came off, but I was thankful that the other half of the piercing had remained in my nose and the newly pierced hole had not closed up.

I contacted my friend, who had, just days before, shoved this piece of metal into my nose. She was sure to inform me that I had nothing to worry about since the stud was still in place. She went on to tell me that all I would have to do is stop by a parlor in St. Louis, buy a new piece, and they would fix it for me there in the shop. She even went as far as to recommend which shop she felt would do the best job. She was right.

Walking into the parlor, I felt as though I was entering into a realm of coolness far beyond my ability to achieve. I could have cashed in all my "cool points," gone out and begged on the streets for more, and I still would not have had enough points to reach beyond the mercy rule.

All around me were these tattoo-covered, heavy-rimmed glasses-wearing, perfectly dressed individuals. In the background, Frank Sinatra was playing. Where had my trusted friend sent me? How did she think I would ever find a place in this crowd? Why on earth are they going to want to go out of their way to help somebody like me?

I know, I know. Insecurity 101. But that's how I felt in the moment.

When I had first walked into this parlor, I had this whole scenario set up in my mind. I thought...these guys are going to think they are so badass. They are going to think they are so much cooler than me (and I am thinking, they're probably right). I am going to go in, explain myself, and in return they are going to be completely fake with me and likely mock me behind my back while their guy is fixing my "stupid problem." *Look at that stupid hipster kid with the nose piercing, begging us to fix it*, is how I envisioned it all playing out in my head.

If there were a movie scene created to play out exactly what I envisioned them to all be like, they would have been pictured as some of the worst people on the planet. I had typecast them as a royal family of douchebags. (But again, this is all premature thinking.)

When I finally got out of my head and entered into the actual parlor, I was greeted with what appeared to be more than just a typical, generic greeting. "Hey, man. Welcome! How are you doing? What can we do for you?" Okay, that sounds generic, but it was packaged with genuineness!

I explained what had happened and just as my friend had informed me, the "cool kids" confirmed that all I would need to do was buy one of their nose pieces and they would have their piercer fix it for me.

And that is exactly what I did.

Looking back, I now realize that I was to them the very thing that I had labeled them to be to me. I was the one that in my head treated them unkindly. They, however, welcomed me in a sincere and genuine manner. They not only fixed my problem, but they did it with style and class. Everything about them seemed authentic. They went out of their way to make me feel like I was worth their respect.

I realize how crazy this sounds, but...I am thankful to have lost my ball on that fateful morning in St. Louis. I think it is safe to say that I was sent to that tattoo parlor to learn an important lesson about stereotyping. If I were going to meet and inspire people in my travels, how could I truly do that while labeling and categorizing them in my own head?

So I say: Talk to anyone and everyone that you can. Not just those who fit into your clean little bubble. Get to know people. Listen to the stories of others on completely different paths of life than you. We all stereotype, so stop kidding yourself. Don't allow that mental weed to take over and direct your life. Do not miss out on potentially life-changing encounters because of what your head is saying.

Stop being a jerk. Stop stereotyping.

.

- ZOEY -

I was on my way to Kentucky when I decided to stop at the halfway mark of my trip and have lunch with some old friends from college. After eating, we all said our "see you laters" and I prepared to leave. I was sitting in my car and putting an address into my GPS, so it would properly direct me to my next stop. To my left, I could see one of my friends doing something in her car. She seemed to be rummaging through her things. When she appeared to find what she was looking for, she quickly headed in my direction. She had a smile on her face. She always did. She was sweet like that.

As she approached my car with her bright eyes and signature smile, I could tell she was up to something. With her fist tightly bound, she extended her hand toward me, in an attempt to hand me something. She gave me a gift. Her gift was meaningful. Her gift was endearing. Her gift was heartfelt. And...her gift was intended to help me on my journey.

After receiving this gift (if your curiosity is getting the best of you, it was a $100 bill) I expressed my deepest thanks for her kindness. We then transitioned into some small talk. I hadn't seen her in nearly ten years and it was great having an opportunity to catch up. So much had changed since the last time I'd seen her. She was a grown woman now, she was a wife, and she was a mother of not just one, but two beautiful babies.

I don't exactly remember how, but we began talking about her children. I told her of my love for the name Zoey, the name she had chosen for her oldest child. We then began talking about the meaning of that name and how it translates in Greek to the word "life." She then shared a very personal story with me about the reasoning for choosing such a name.

She told me of how she and her husband saw Zoey for the very first time, before she was born. At only nine weeks old, Zoey was just this tiny little life form, no bigger than a gummy bear, in the stomach of her mother. She told me how you could already see a little body beginning to develop: little arms and legs beginning to show themselves and even a head starting to form. She went on to tell me that, as tiny as this little piece of life was, Zoey was living large and loud as they watched on the screen while she danced in the stomach of her mother.

Zoey, at a mere nine weeks, moved around in a lively fashion as they watched. She was moving her arms and legs, and making it known that she was indeed alive. Zoey was living as loud as she possibly could, as if to say, "This is me! I may be little, but I will not go unnoticed!"

In that moment, while I listened to this story, I found myself connecting with what may have been a hidden moral. I'm no fool to the way this thing called life works. I am aware that there will be (and have been) times when

I will feel small in comparison to all that is happening around me. Much like Zoey, at times I have felt like I am the size of a gummy bear and that everything around me is so much larger and even more overwhelming. There are times when I feel like I am unable to do much of anything due to these feelings of insignificance in the vastness of this world. Such feelings often attempt to keep me from doing what I feel I am meant to do. But, if I truly believe that I am unimportant, and simply not cool enough to talk to the people I meet, then my story, no matter how great, will be ineffective.

And the lesson that I learned was this: If an infant nine weeks in utero and only an inch long is capable of representing the fullness of life, then I am, too. I can live loudly. I can stand tall and strong, full of passion, knowing that all I have to do is wave my arms and legs around and say, "My name is Cooper! This is my story, and I am very much full of life!"

-MASON JARS ARE SEXY-

She was sitting at the table directly next to mine. She looked like somebody I could connect with. She had dark hair and rimmed glasses. Her outfit was trendy and she seemed somewhat artsy. She was also super cute. Actually, she was pretty hot.

I knew that my reason for being on this journey was not to meet girls, but at that moment I still found myself wanting to do something that I naturally like to do… flirt!

I have to admit, I had been "out of the game" for some time. I was apprehensive to pull the trigger because I felt as though I had lost my ability to "talk" to girls. I tried not to give off a creepy vibe as I continued checking her out. She was reading. I don't know why, but the reading made her hotter. As I looked over at her for probably the eleventy-seventh time, I noticed that she was drinking her coffee from a Mason jar. The coffee I ordered came in a *cup*. A boring coffee mug. Where did she get a Mason jar? Does coffee taste better from a Mason jar?

I decided to just go for it. I looked over at her and I said something from my actual lips rather than just in my head. "Hey, so uh…does it taste better that way?" She looked up. Clearly she knew that I was talking to her since she was the only one anywhere close to me. She was polite, but she looked somewhat confused. "I'm sorry?" she replied. *Maybe I should have just kept talking to her in my head,* I thought to myself. It was easier that way. I replied, "Oh, I was wondering if it tastes better that way? You know, the coffee?" I pointed to the Mason jar. I tried to make it obvious that I was being funny. She smiled and said, "I don't know, probably not any different," with a cute little laugh.

Perhaps it was a pity laugh, but I knew she had taken the bait nonetheless. I knew that I had her attention. I decided to keep talking, except this time...I spoke in a different language. That's right, I am trilingual. Impressive, right? I proudly profess to speak in the languages of: English, sarcasm, and small talk.

I busted out my small talk ability and to my surprise, I discovered that she too was a speaker of the language.

I started off with the basics. I asked her about her work. She told me she was a theater teacher. My mental list was growing: she is super cute, has great style, reads books, drinks from Mason jars, and she is into performing arts? *Okay Cooper,* I thought to myself. *This is only week two. You are not on this journey to find girls. Stay focused, Cooper. Stay. Focused.*

My new ~~girl~~friend continued to tell me about her job, and about the opportunity to take her passion for art and theater and travel to different schools and educate students. Her job was interesting and always changing because she was never in one school for much more than a week or two. She was able to share her passion with a variety of students in a variety of places. She was a nomadic theater instructor who drank coffee from a Mason jar. This girl. She was not making this easy on me.

She went on to tell me how she appreciated the ability to do all of the things that she loved and also share that love with so many others. This was inspiring to me. What she was describing was essentially what I found myself doing. I was in the very beginning of my journey and I had already found a like-minded person. And she was living out her dreams so successfully. I was passionate about storytelling. I was driven by the people that I would share my story with. I had the desire to inspire others simply by doing the things that I love most.

So why did I meet this woman? Did we cross paths for a specific reason? Did the fact that I was feeling as though my choice to share my story and spread hope across the country (rather than getting a real job and spending my time "working") might not be the right one have something to do with our meeting? Was my morning purposely interrupted by someone doing something similar to show me that it was possible? Was she here to let me know that I was not wasting my time?

If nothing else, she motivated me. She helped to form the foundation on which I would build my journey. She let me know that there are other people in this world sharing their passions in less than ordinary ways. She was also ridiculously cute. Whether coincidence or destiny, I am thankful to have met her.

Oh...and one thing is for certain: Mason jars are sexy.

-THE TOY TRAIN-

A simple toy train: that was all it took to make his world go around. He was only three and he loved them.

I saw him play with these toy trains every day. He had wooden tracks that he would carefully put together for them to run along. He wore shirts that featured trains. He watched YouTube clips about trains. He basically ate, drank, and breathed trains. He wanted to see them, touch them, and experience them. And he wanted to share that experience with everyone else, too.

I remember hearing him wake up each morning, and before anything else, he would ask his mother for his toy trains.

I remember returning home after a long day spent visiting coffee shops and hearing him ask his dad to play trains with him.

One of the things that intrigued me the most was his knowledge of these trains. At such a young age, he could tell you parts, positions, and specific purposes of specific cars. He was brilliant.

If he was asked to wait patiently until it was time to play with his trains, he did so (most of the time; I mean...he was a little boy). He loved them so much that he was willing to do whatever he was asked in order to experience their greatness once again. It was clearly never an easy task for him, but because of his love for them, he put everything he had into doing what he needed to see them once again.

If you promised him that you would play trains with him at a later time, you better not forget it. He certainly wouldn't.

This little guy could only function in a world where trains existed. He didn't know anything different. He didn't want to.

After experiencing a week with my train-loving buddy, I left wondering...what is my "train"? Am I that passionate about something? Have I devoted my life to something that others can plainly see when they look at me?

When I began my journey, it was my desire to share hope with the people that I met. Sure, he was only a three-year-old boy, but maybe he (and his trains) were teaching me a lesson on how to be passionate about my purpose.

I needed (and if I am honest, still need) to learn how to eat, drink, and breathe the *hope* that I set out to share. When people see me, they should notice the anticipation in my eyes before they notice the scar running down my neck. Hope should seep from my pores.

But, why do I so often fail at this? Why do I lose focus? Why do I allow myself to get distracted? Why am I unable to stay in that place where *hope* is my all, my only, and my everything?

I think too much. I allow myself to live in the past. I dwell on things that I can't control in the future. And as a result, I miss out on living in the now, which in conclusion robs me of experiencing the joy that comes from my most "favoritest" toy train.

-PEZ MAN-

Never had I seen so many toys. And I wasn't in a toy store, or even a child's playroom. I was in a grown man's room—a *big* grown man. He towered over me in height. He had the voice of Goliath. Things in the room rumbled when he spoke. The ground shook when he walked. He looked like he belonged on an Olympic rugby team, and...he played with toys? Okay, he actually did not play with them, but he "collected" them. This concept has always been weird to me. Sure, you keep it in the box and eventually it will be valuable later...blah, blah, blah, but I just don't get it. When I was a kid and I bought any toy, the last thing I wanted to do was keep it in the box! As soon as I got that thing, I couldn't wait to rip that baby open and play with it!

My large, new friend "the collector" had a special fascination with Pez dispensers. I know, right? Pez! Those plastic, spring-loaded containers with the head on top, which distributes what may be one of the most disgusting candies created by mankind. Even as a child I couldn't stand the colorful little pill-shaped "candy." I partook of them once or twice in my lifetime, but *only* because my curiosity got the best of me. I would see them staring me down in the checkout lane each and every time I went to the grocery store with my mother. And every time that I did give in to their pull on me, I was *always* disappointed. Each and every time I ate those things, it was like consuming the Brussels sprouts of candies. Talk about a total letdown when you're just a kid.

Standing in the room of my new friend, I could not help but be baffled. However, I would never belittle this beast of a man and his apparent obsession. I stand at a mere five foot eight and on a good day, I might weigh 150 pounds. As far as this Goliath was concerned, I thought that Pez was the coolest thing on the planet. I went along with his "tour de Pez" even though none of it made any sense to me. He showed me this dispenser and that dispenser, recalling the story behind each of them. He told me about the first dispenser he ever owned and he showed me his most recent acquisition. I smiled and nodded, doing the best I could to seem interested. Honestly, I kept waiting for Ashton Kutcher to come out of a closet and say, "You've been punked!" but it never happened.

Before entering his room, I had expected to be met with "man stuff." I was prepared for *Sports Illustrated*, weight benches, and his collection of seasonal, city, sport-league jerseys. Instead, there was...Pez?

He had dispensers displayed on specially made shelves, books about different dispensers, and Pez valuation catalogs. He told me stories about his friends who would frequently call him after seeing dispensers they weren't sure if he had or not. It had become somewhat of a game for them—they wanted to find the missing piece to his puzzle. I was completely caught off guard by this entire experience and began to wonder, how can I relate to this? How do I connect with this person?

I obviously have no interest whatsoever in collecting candy-holding plastic head things, but I do have a desire for people to look at my life and see that I am different. I often speak loudly about my "non-conformist ways." I boast that I am an "individualistic sort of guy," not seeking to do what is "cool," but rather doing my own thing.

I make it my point to inform others that I know who I am and I do not worry or care what others think.

But, if I am completely truthful, I also realize how desperately I attempt to be accepted at times. So often, I feel this strong need to "fit in" and be what everyone expects or wants me to be.

Though the situation seemed strange, I am thankful to have met the Pez-Man. He was not ashamed to be who he was, even if it went against what would socially be considered "normal." He didn't fit into the typical "tough guy" stereotype, and he was unapologetic. He was strange and different...and I liked him.

He also had a network of friends, who went out of their way to help him improve his collection. They hoped to bring something to him that would be special and valuable to only him. They were his support system. They did not see an awkward, grown man collecting toys. They saw a friend with a passion.

At the root of Coffee with Cooper was my desire to share pieces of myself with others. I wanted them to see my passions. I wanted to catch them off guard. Pez-Man so simply helped me remember that I do not have to be ashamed to be who I am. I am a guy living life one day at a time. I am a Christian. I am socially awkward. I wear my heart on my sleeve. I am a person who makes mistakes, but tries to allow them to help me grow. I am a cancer survivor. I am divorced. I am imperfect. I am a recovering alcoholic. I am a work in progress. I am something in the making. I am...human.

-THE NOT SO KOREAN KOREANS-

When my host in Louisville told me the news, I was ecstatic. She wanted me to meet her Korean friends. She told me she had invited a family over to have a meal with us. She also mentioned that she had informed her friends that prior to my cancer diagnosis, I lived in Korea for nearly two years.

Prior to my official diagnosis I had spent twenty months teaching English in South Korea. I thought I was going to be there for five years. It wasn't until I found myself starting to get sick, visiting some Korean doctors, and being informed that I more than likely had cancer, that I even considered coming back to America.

I love Korea. I loved living there. I loved the people. I loved my job (most days). I loved the culture. And I loved the food. Since moving back home, I found myself missing the culture and craving the food. When I heard that there would be a real-life Korean family and a meal, I suddenly felt like a kid on Christmas morning.

Only one thing worried me about meeting my soon-to-be Korean friends. It was something that I am rather ashamed to admit. While I may have lived in Korea for nearly two years, I actually failed miserably at picking up the language. Upon arriving in Korea, I had the greatest intentions of learning the language, but a problem arose when all of the friends that I made already spoke English. I am saddened to say that my desire to pick up the language faded quickly. I did manage to pick up a few common phrases, but most days I was able to get by in my native tongue.

After my first year in Korea, I recalled my original intent to learn the language, and I started checking into options to do just that. I was excited to find that I could take language courses at a university in the city where I lived. My excitement quickly turned to sadness when I learned that I had missed the deadline to sign up. When the next sign-up period came around, I had already started getting sick and was heading back to the United States.

Though my excitement for a real "Korean Weekend" was overwhelming, I was embarrassed to face my soon-to-be friends and not be able to carry on even a simple conversation in Korean.

Earlier on this particular day, I was asked to make a list of things I wanted to eat for dinner. I was informed that the friends would be picking up dinner, and I was to pick out some dishes that everyone might like. You know, since I was the Korean "expert."

I came up with a list of options that I thought would make an enjoyable dinner for everyone. I suggested:

Jajangmyeon (which is actually a Korean Chinese dish) is noodles with a black bean paste that usually includes vegetables and pork. These noodles were one of my very absolute favorite things to eat.

Samgyeopsal: This is thinly sliced pieces of pork belly that are grilled. Oftentimes there will be some spices and fresh garlic to add into the mix. This is an excellent choice if you are ever in a position to have some.

Galbi: This is a marinated or seasoned beef that, like Samgyeopsal, you grill. It is essentially a Korean BBQ. It's truly amazing!

Dak galbi: This is a mixture of rice cakes, spicy red sauce, cabbage, rice, and chicken. I actually did not enjoy this meal (at all) when I first arrived in Korea, but I could not get enough of it by the time I left.

After that, my list was complete, and I was convinced there would be something for everyone.

When my new friends arrived, I liked them right away. All of them were happy and outgoing in their own unique way. They were not the kind of people that appeared to be superficial or fake because they had just met you. You could easily tell that they were genuinely kind people.

Despite the linguistic embarrassment lingering in the back of my mind, I was excited for a night of Korean fun...in America. As we began to set the table, I was informed that the Korean restaurant only served one of the dishes I had suggested. I was a little sad, a bit baffled that they did not serve more of the meals that I loved, but excited for the food nonetheless.

We began digging into the galbi, as well as all of the side dishes that restaurant had provided. Everyone seemed to enjoy their food and conversations came easily. I learned about my friends and how some of the family was unable to make it that night due to work. I was so thrilled to hear about their lives, but they were more interested in hearing about my time in Korea. I told them about my first year in the country, how I lived in a very small village and worked at a local elementary school. I described my transition from there to a much larger city for my second year. Wonju was actually the largest city in the province of Gangwon-do, and I called it my home for nearly a year.

As I spoke of my days overseas, every now and then I would slip in one of the few Korean words or phrases that I knew. I also spoke of specific cities and landmarks. In these moments, I never got any sort of immediate response. I thought that maybe it was my accent (or lack thereof); I was probably butchering the language and they were more than likely being polite.

When this occurred multiple times, I became curious enough to pursue the topic on my own. I asked if the children were bilingual, assuming to hear "Yes!" and have them share their linguistic skills with me. But, no! Actually, the children were not bilingual. They spoke almost no Korean at all. I came to find out that the mother of my new friends had been adopted at a very early age. She was so young that she quickly forgot any and all of the Korean she knew. Since she had lived in America most of her life and married an American man, she never really had a reason to learn Korean.

My new friends were basically these not-so-Korean Koreans—this knowledge cleared up any and all confusion that had clouded my thoughts. This is why there were not any responses to my very brief usage of the Korean language. This is why they didn't know most of the places I spoke of.

I admit that I had a ton of premature, unfair expectations of my new friends. Once the weight of worry was lifted off my shoulders, I actually felt a little cool! It was as if I were the "Caucasian Korean" that could answer most all of their questions. Despite my lack of the language, I was a Korean expert!

Prior to this meal, I had expected my Korean friends to judge me because I didn't know much Korean, but they didn't. Not even close.

I think I do that a lot in life. I often have these premature thoughts about the people that I meet, or even those I already know. I assume they are going to judge me for some reason and devalue me as a person. I fear they'll get to know me and then find a reason to not want to continue investing into me. I didn't learn Korean after living in Korea for nearly two years... So what? That doesn't make me stupid! And my friends still wanted to invest in me nonetheless.

I shouldn't expect that other people will be so judgmental. I shouldn't doubt myself and project that doubt onto others. It's like I'm prejudging myself from *their* perspective. These thoughts often consume me. They imprison me. They cause me to miss out on the fullness of true relationships and experience the community developed through life.

I am thankful that I met my Korean friends. They unknowingly opened my eyes to my harmful behavior. This awakening didn't repair the problem, of course, but it left me with an opportunity and desire to change. I need to work on my perception of others. And I need to work on me and how I treat *myself* in the confinement of my own head.

Oh, and I really need to learn more Korean.

-FRUIT-FULL-

S ome people have never been to Europe. Some have never smoked a cigarette. Others have never flown on a plane. We all encounter life in our own way, so differences are natural and expected. I was never shocked by a single "Never have I ever..." statement until the encounter which left me retrieving pieces of my mind off the floor (as a result of it being *blown*).

You'd think I was visiting a far-off place. Maybe I was in Papua New Guinea, or some remote corner of the world where access is limited. But I wasn't. I was in the first-world country where I was born and raised. I was in a room surrounded by familiar faces when I learned of one person's total lack of experience in such a normal part of life for the general population of the entire planet.

She had never had an orange.

This is not even a joke. I kid you not.

I was dumbfounded. To be completely honest, I thought that my friends were just messing with me. But, as they continued to talk, I realized that we were actually dealing with a real-life, fruit-sheltered individual. I was forced to realize that I really have not seen it all.

There she stood: a Midwestern girl, born and raised. She was also a scholar and a recent college graduate. She had experienced much in her twenty-two years on earth, but somehow...her lips had never experienced its amazingness. Somehow her tongue had never tasted its wonder.

Why? Her actual reasoning was...the texture looks icky, so the flavor must be sicky. (I realize that sicky is not a word, but you get the point. She thought they would taste bad!)

Why!? I wondered. Why would she ever think that!? I know that this is not true. Obviously, you (the reader) know that this is not true. The entire population of mankind from the past, present, and future knows that this is not true. Yet, this girl had allowed herself to be so mentally misguided.

I think it's safe to say that every person in the room felt the same way as we stood there listening to her talk about her awful lifestyle choices. Up to this point, she had quite simply led a fruitless life. The absence of orange was truly appalling. We all desperately wanted to make a difference in her life and help her make a change for the better.

As with many righteous fights, it only took one passionate person to stand up for the cause and get the ball of momentum rolling in the right direction. And that day it only took that one person to take a stand and say, "I will give her an orange."

Anxiously we all stood in silence as our friend stood with the missing link in her hand. We all desired the same results, but respectfully allowed her to make her own decisions. Slowly and reluctantly, she pulled it toward her mouth. With fear and uncertainty in the depths of her eyes, she brought the piece closer and closer. We all watched with anticipation as she placed the piece of fruit in her mouth and chewed.

It was like watching a mother hold her child for the first time. It was like finding that missing puzzle piece you needed to complete the masterpiece puzzle. It was like hearing your friend tell you she is getting married.

In these moments, there really are no words to best describe the realness. But, we didn't need words to understand, because her eyes said it all.

She was fruitfully complete.

-THE SWINDLER-

Prior to beginning the journey I didn't have a vehicle. Thankfully I was able to find a used car at a very cheap price. It was an old-school vehicle. A '92 Lincoln Town Car. I knew it would suck the gas like a child does a milkshake, but I didn't care. I had myself a car! Emphasis on the "had." The motor blew less than a month after I bought it. As it turns out, that little red light that shows you an oilcan, it really does mean "check your oil." And, if you don't check your oil while you have a small leak, all of it leaks out. This results in a catastrophe known as, your motor blowing.

But...I'd be lying if I said that was the craziest part of this story.

You should know by now that the concept of Coffee with Cooper is one that parallels my personality in a number of ways. When the thought of it happening began to surface, I was overwhelmed with joy. I was ecstatic. When my motor blew, I became very discouraged, but I did not lose heart. I quickly put together what I felt was an honest and worthy fundraiser and watched as many of my friends and followers contributed funds. I was beyond encouraged.

My cup was overflowing. I knew, I just knew, that everything was going to work out.

Every day I would search for a vehicle within my meager price range. I scoured the internet and I had a few people talking to friends at car lots. I looked, and I looked, and I test drove, and I looked. None of the cars that I found gave me the feeling of security I would need to have if I were going to drive a vehicle across the country. The departure date for my trip was drawing closer, and I was beginning to feel a little desperate, when I received a message from a person I had been acquainted with in the past. This person will remain nameless because...well...I'm a nice guy. What he did to me was wrong and deceitful.

The message opened with a voice of concern about my current dealings with cancer. The concern was followed with sympathy, because the nameless person had family members who had dealt with bad bouts of cancer. The conversation soon transitioned into him telling me that he wanted to help me. He went on to say that he felt "called" to do something kind for me. He informed me that he believed in what I was attempting to do with CWC, and wanted to play a role in helping make it happen. He currently had a car for sale. It was a reliable car worth $4,400 and he would be willing to sell it to me for $2,250! I was blown away. I had fruitlessly searched high and low for a car within my budget and here was someone who wanted to take a car far beyond my reach and put me behind the wheel. I felt encouraged. I felt blessed. This trip was going to happen!

As we continued talking about the details of the car, and how I would need to fly out to Colorado to pick it up, he texted me about a concern he was beginning to have. He felt like $2,250 was a really great deal—too great—and now he was thinking that it would be more fair to him if we considered $2,500. He reminded me of the fact that the car was worth $4,400 and that I was still getting an amazing deal. I remember him even using the phrase "I don't want there to be bad blood between us." This was the first of many red flags that should have alarmed me, but failed to. I guess all I was thinking was that this person *really* did want to help me and that regardless of the first or second price, I really was getting a great deal.

We then began discussing how I could come pick up the car. He actually offered to fly me out to Colorado and pick me up at the airport! I was so impressed. Not only did he want to give me a good deal on this car, but now he was willing to fly me out! I naturally assumed that this meant, "I am prepared to pay for your ticket," so, I did what I felt was normal and began searching for flights. I found one for $190, which I felt was very reasonable. I messaged him to let him know the details. "Okay, I have a flight credit for $50," he said. "Will that work?" I won't lie…I was confused. Why would he tell me that he would "fly me out there" when his intention was actually to contribute to flying me out there with his $50 flight credit? I suppose any contribution should not go unnoted. As it turned out, the credit was for an airline that charged far more than $190 for the ticket, so I decided against using it altogether. So much for that gesture of kindness.

I had a budget to stick to if I was going to make this work. I now had to pay to fly out there, pay for the car itself, and pay for gas to get back to my original destination. I had worked hard to save funds, and many others had donated their own money to fund my car purchase. If this trip out there was going to dissolve a lot of those funds then it would not benefit me.

So with the car now priced at $2,500 plus the $190 for my flight, plus the cost of the gas I would need to travel to my first destination (St. Louis) from Colorado Springs, I was spreading myself a little thin. But…I thought I could make it work. The one thing I was really thankful for was the fact that he was going to allow me to stay at his place the night I picked up the car, instead of me having to spend money on a hotel. This would allow me to rest before the very long drive ahead of me.

One day before my departure to Colorado, I received another message from my "friend." The message basically said, "My dad says I am selling the car too cheap, I am going to need $3,000." I was a bit startled. Okay, I was completely shocked. What!? I already bought my plane ticket! I know what you are thinking: Whew, good thing he got out of that deal before he handed over all of his money! But I am sorry to tell you that is not what happened. I know I should have been seeing all of these red flags (there were so many waving in my face at this point) but the passion that consumes my heart for CWC got the best of me. I told him that I would see what I could do. I eventually had to let him know that I was unable to come up with any more money at this point. He then told me to go ahead and make the trip out, and that we would "arrange something." So that's what I did. I hopped on the plane to Colorado, and when my friend picked me up in the car that would soon be mine, I had my $2,500 ready.

Before heading to Colorado, we had discussed how the transaction would occur. We had been having this conversation via Facebook and text messaging. He requested that when I came I'd bring cash to pay for the car. I told him that I would not bring cash. I informed him that I did not want to carry that much cash, and that I'd also need some sort of proof that I had given him money. I believe this was my one smart move, my saving grace, at the beginning stages of this whole ordeal. He began getting upset when I told him I couldn't bring cash to pay for this car. I then suggested that we take the route of cashier's check. He voiced his concern about this process, and insisted that a cashier's check would not work since my bank was in a different state. I told him that his bank would be happy to cash it, to which he replied, "But my bank is in another state!" What? Your bank is in another state than the one you live in? And again, bright red flag smacking me in the face...but I just let it fly. I decided that getting money orders through Walmart would be our best and only option. I informed him that I would get the money orders before I left and that I would bring them with me to Colorado. I told him that all he had to do was take these money orders to *any* Walmart and they'd be happy to cash them. He was still a little reluctant, but then called me to let me know that he had called Walmart and was told that my plan would work.

There was also a small title issue, which he was "honest" about upfront. He informed me that, when he purchased the car, he had sent the title off to be replaced so it would be in his name. He said he was still waiting for the replacement title to arrive. He informed me that when I had paid him the remaining $500 for the car he could have the title mailed to me. The tags that were on it did not expire for another year, so as far as getting pulled over was concerned, I was driving a "friend's" car.

When I arrived in Colorado, I had three money orders: one for $500 and two for $1,000. We immediately headed to Walmart with the intention of cashing them. We arrived at Walmart, where it became obvious that this guy was more than ready to have the cash in his hand. Unfortunately, we ran into a mother lode of problems. There was a processing error in the money orders that were made out for $1,000. The $500 money order cleared without any issues, but the other two wouldn't and... didn't. Calls were made to the customer service number and we were basically told that we would need to send the money orders to a bank, where they could then be processed properly. I don't know why this was happening and I honestly didn't think it was that big of a deal. Who needs $2,500 at 8pm anyway?!

At that point, it was late and I was tired. I just wanted to sleep. As we left Walmart, my friend became belligerent. He started screaming and cussing, and throwing an all-out temper tantrum...all while driving down the interstate at an ungodly speed. He occasionally would stop screaming long enough to inform me that he was not mad at me, but he was mad at the situation. He was mad that he didn't get all of his money that night. As far as I was concerned, he did have it all! Sure, it was in money order form, but he had every penny! I did what I could to assert some rational thinking and assure him that things were going to be fine. It soon became obvious that rational thinking had no place in this conversation. He continued to scream, and started saying things like, "I knew I should *not* have done this" and "I knew I should have stuck with my gut" and "I knew I should have told you *all cash* or *nothing!*" Don't worry, though, he was not mad at me, he was only mad at the situation.

I soon realized that he was intoxicated by his desire to have all of that money. In an attempt to appease him, we headed to another Walmart. He believed that there was probably some technical error at the first store, and by going to a different one we would have better results. When the second effort also failed, more screaming and cursing followed. He even went as far as to look at the girl who had told him that it was not going to work and call her a "stupid bitch." As he stormed out, I stood there awkwardly staring back at the two workers who were left staring at me. I apologized profusely and made up excuses for my friend. But the truth is, there was no excuse for what he did. It was wrong, it was rude, and it was a red flag, blazing with fire.

I returned to the car with the strong desire to punch him in the face. I would have loved nothing more than to tell him to get out of my car, but he still had the title. To proceed as anything other than a well-mannered person would have only infuriated him more. So I cautiously spoke, reassuring him that everything was going to be fine, and we would get this issue resolved. His response was to speed down the interstate once again, screaming every curse word known to man.

By then, I was more than ready for that bed he offered. There was a small part of me that was afraid that if I slept at his place, he would murder me in my sleep, but I didn't have money to be spending on a hotel room. As we headed for his home, he began to tell me about his job. He informed me that (don't laugh) he was a counselor. He told me he had his doctorate and he practiced international counseling via Skype. I had heard of counseling being done over Skype, and when I knew him before, I recalled his passion for that field. In a freaked-out sort of way, I believed him. He had gone on to say that some of his patients might Skype him that night, and he would prefer if I were not there when that happened. I thought, well, that's fine. He could just go to his room and I could go to a different room or sleep on the couch or something. He must have a decent room for him to practice his professional job, right? As it turned out, he lived in a motel. He told me that he lived there because he had been "working with" the guy who owned it. He told me that the guy had made a lot of progress, and he continued to stay there because of that relationship. So, he is a doctor who counsels from his hotel room in Colorado Springs. No big deal, right?

He proceeded to tell me that he needed his room to himself. He might have clients call, plus he was really upset about "the situation" and needed to be alone. Thankfully, he offered to pay for my hotel room, because I just didn't have the money to pay for unexpected expenses like that. He called his friend who owned the hotel where he was staying and attempted to get a discounted price on a room, but his friend wanted too much money. We were forced to look for a room somewhere else. We ended up at a place that seemed a tad cheap and somewhat shady, but safe enough for me to stay for the night. Anything away from this guy made me feel safe! We went inside, where he asked the woman behind the counter if she had a room available for the night. She said that she did, and stated that the cost would be approximately $50. My friend scoffed then tossed a $20 bill on the counter. He turned to me and told me that I could cover the rest. I wanted nothing more than to punch him in the face repeatedly. But it was more than obvious I was the only rational one between the two of us, so a swift beating, no matter how appealing, would not have benefited me at all. I reluctantly paid the remaining balance. I would have done whatever it took at that point to get away from him. I wanted to get him the rest of his money and never have to speak to him again. Ever. I had my car, he had his money, and we had an agreement for the remainder. (Since it had been revealed to me before my arrival that they would need $3,000 instead of the original $2,500, we had worked out a payment plan. I would pay $50 a month to them through PayPal for ten months. Until I paid the other $500 that had been requested, I would not be getting the title.) I went to my room, locked my door (he had heard my room number, after all), got into bed, and fell asleep.

The next morning, I was pumped! I finally had the car that I needed and I was about to embark on this amazing journey. A couple of hours down the road, I received a text message: "Hey, Coop. Please don't forget to put the $50 a month into my paypal account that we agreed on." I assured him that I would follow through with my part of the deal and that everything would be fine.

My trip continued on as planned. Coffee with Cooper was finally happening! St. Louis was a blast! Louisville was amazing! Nashville was wonderful! I was two days from my departure to Birmingham when I got a message: "Coop, my dad is going to report the car stolen. You need to get it back here now!" In that moment, I am pretty sure my jaw hit the floor. He said that if I just paid the $500 that I owed him right now, his dad would not call the police. He went on to say, "$1,000 would be better, but I know you don't have that." After a lot of confused texting, I discovered that this car I had purchased and been driving did *not* belong to the person I purchased it from. It belonged to his father.

A lot of people ask (and a lot more probably wonder), did you get a bill of sale or a receipt or make a contract or anything? All of these are fair questions, but the answer to all of them is…sadly…foolishly…no. I guess I was going on the honor system. This guy is someone I knew in the past. We had similar interests, similar friends, and he has family who has dealt with cancer. He told me that he really believed in my project. I thought he really cared. I thought I could trust him.

I was struck with disappointment and fear. I had no idea what to do. I talked the situation over with the host family that I was staying with that week. I explained the details of the story, including the newest developments. As I continued to talk it through, I found myself exposing some details that I hadn't considered important before that moment. The man who sold me the car was a recovering gambling addict. When he had originally approached me with the offer for the car, he used his recovery from addiction to connect with me. He told me that he had overcome this obstacle and as a recovering addict myself (from other things, not gambling), I took him at his word.

I was so upset. All I wanted to do was come to some sort of a solution that would end with the title in my hand. I considered trying to take out a loan from a friend for $500 so that I could give him the money and just be done with it all. But my Nashville hosts, in all of their wisdom, begged me not to give the seller any more money. They recommended that I ask to talk to the father directly. The seller was persistent, and continued to recommend that I mail him a check for the remaining $500 as soon as possible. He assured me that he would then send that check to his father in Illinois. Then, his father would send the title to Colorado to be put in his name, and he would sign it over to me. I was assured that everything would be just fine, but I really needed to hurry up and mail him the money or his father would call the cops.

Per the advice of my friends, I tried to get the phone number of the father. I even found and messaged a person on Facebook who I thought might be the father. When I did not receive a response, I started to believe that maybe my "friend" was telling the truth. Maybe the father *had* reported the car stolen.

I was running out of options, when I came up with a plan. (You will have to forgive me for lying, but sometimes these situations require a well-placed lie.) I wrote the seller a note. I told him that my uncle had agreed to help me out with the $500, but only under certain conditions. I said that my uncle had loaned me money in the past, but I had failed to pay him back in a timely manner. I told him that my uncle was unwilling to place any more money in my hand. The only way he would agree to help me again is if he could write a check directly to the father. I told him that my uncle would even deliver it to his father, since he would be passing through the area where his father lived. I explained that this was a win-win situation: the father would get the money, and I would get the title right away. I received a response rather quickly. In short, the dude flipped out. He f-bombed my "stupid plan" and my uncle. He went on and on about how he would not let some crazy old man (my uncle) near his father.

It became rather clear rather quickly that I was being conned. He had taken my money—all of the money that I saved and that had been gifted to me for my trip. He was now using the title and threatening calls to the cops as leverage to make and get more money; money that I didn't even have. I knew that my trip could not continue until the situation was resolved. I made a tough decision and left Nashville early. I headed back to St. Louis, where Coffee with Cooper began. I knew that I needed to be close to home to properly take care of this, though I had no idea what "taking care of this" even consisted of. Uncertain and afraid, I went back home.

I had a circle of friends in the city with whom I shared the recent development. As word passed through the grapevine, I actually got a call from a guy I knew back in the day. He wanted to share some information with me. He knew for a fact that the swindler's dad had not called the cops, nor was he planning to. He knew this because he was a friend of the swindler and even a friend of the father. He informed me that the father was a man with good intentions, who was more upset at his son for selling his car than anything. He also gave me the father's phone number so that we could discuss the issue.

My friend was right. The father was a decent guy. I was able to call and speak candidly with him about the entire situation. He adamantly told me not to give the vehicle back to his son. He also told me not to give him another dime. He confirmed that the title was still in his possession and that once he received the $1,700 his son still owed him for the car he would sign the title directly over to me. I informed him that I had already paid $2,500 for the car, and was in the process of making monthly payments to pay off the remaining $500. I told him that I didn't understand why he had not received his portion of the money (the $1,700 that he was owed). We came to the conclusion together that the money I had given his son for the car was already gone. It had been gambled away.

I have no desire to drag my "friend" through the dirt. I do not wish to poke fun at his, or anyone else's, struggle with addiction. I was deeply saddened. This guy took advantage of me. He took advantage of my faith in humanity, my illness, and my desire to make a change in the world around me. He took these things and used them to get my $2,500. That was the goal, and he had scored. And...he was still out for more.

Sadly, I wasn't the only victim in this situation. This guy sold out his own father by selling a car that he did not rightfully own. The whole reason that the dad became lean holder of the title was to help his child. He attempted to prevent him from doing exactly what he ultimately did and in the end he manipulated me and he stole from his father.

Unfortunately, the messages from my old "friend" continued to fill my inbox. "I will call the cops Cooper, you have no legal right to that car." Other times it was "I know you talked to my dad. Just do whatever he said, Coop." Or "Coop, keep the car. All is forgiven. Just pay my dad the other $500 and he can mail you the title." And soon we were right back to, "You better pay me the money or else I'll call the cops!" I attempted to keep up with the never-ending saga, but it wore on me. Every morning and sometimes during the day, I'd receive and attempt to respond to these threatening messages. At one point I even said, "You can have the car. Come out here and get it, and give me my money back. I will take cash or a money order." In response, I was told that the car had been reported stolen, and there was a warrant out for my arrest. But don't worry, because eight hours later he sent me a message that read, "We are cool man. No worries. Just pay my dad."

Eventually, I just stopped responding.

I called the father again. I apologized for what his son had put him through. I let him know that I understood that both of us had been duped, and I asked if he would be willing to work with me to resolve the situation once and for all. I told him that I understood my money was gone forever, but I still felt like he should get his. If he would make a deal with me (in writing and notarized) I would be willing to pay him installments to pay off the $1,700 that his child still owed him. I offered to pay nine installments of $189. He counter-offered with ten installments of $100.

I was thrilled. Whether I paid him $1,700 or $1,000, I was still going to come out ahead on the value of the car vs. what I paid. I was thankful for and encouraged by the father's willingness to work with me. I know that most people would say I did not owe this guy a dime, and honestly I would agree with you. But this was a chance for me to show grace to a person who probably hadn't seen a whole lot in his lifetime. This was a chance for me to make a little good out of a bad situation.

So I met up with the father of the swindler. I took him a contract that I had made up (the one that my uncle was going to deliver, haha) and we signed and notarized it there. He was such a great man and he became a great source of encouragement for me. We even ended up having dinner together and he shared powerful stories of his past with me. He told me that he had met and beat cancer *four* times!

Two payments into my ten-payment plan I received a message from the swindler's father. It read something to the effect of, "Why don't you just pay me $300 more and we'll call it even." That meant I only had to pay the original $500 more! What a solid man that swindler's father turned out to be!

-WE AIN'T GOT NO MONEY, BUT WE'VE SURE GOT LOVE-

They struggled to make ends meet, but they survived, one day at a time. They scrounged up every penny possible to pay their bills and put food on the table. Both worked hard at their mediocre jobs. As hard as they worked, they had fallen a little behind on rent. Actually, they had fallen a lot behind. They hadn't yet lost their home, but they were beginning to wonder how long the extended period of grace from their landlord would last.

They did their best to carry on with life as if nothing were wrong. Their faces held smiles and their struggles were successfully concealed. They seemed truly happy. I can honestly say that this happiness was, in no way, forced. It was something they dug to the deepest parts of their hearts to find. I knew nothing of their money troubles until days after my arrival in their home.

As I sat and talked with my dear friend, she exposed these troubles. I could hear the worry in her voice. She wondered what they would do if their landlord ran out of patience. Where would they go? She liked her job and her friends. This place was her home, and she had no desire to move. As she spoke, she fought for strength, but her exhaustion was beginning to show. I so understood having to deal with both uncertainty and concern. God knows I had lived with trials of my own. Rather than share my personal struggles, I took the opportunity that night to listen. I recalled the advice my friend (whom I had the very first CWC conversation with from St. Louis) had given me when my mouth was full of food and I desperately wanted to give answers to all of her questions: *Don't talk, just eat*, I remembered her saying. Only, in this situation, I told myself, don't talk, just listen.

Throughout the rest of my week, I carried the weight of my friends' difficulties, but I was also inspired by their persistence. I kept thinking about how hard this couple worked. Regardless of their circumstances, they steered straight. They weren't broken and battered. They were not frantic. The pair was bold and strong. I believe their positivity was driven by their children, who they allowed to live in blissful ignorance of their monetary situation.

My friends were obviously amazing, so I shouldn't have been surprised by the level of awesome displayed by their children. All of the kids were respectful and kind. Each one exhibited a surprising amount of maturity and integrity. I have no doubt that these traits were a direct result of their parents' example. Selfless. Perseverant. Loving. Faithful. Influential. Amidst chaos, they set their children up for nothing less than success.

While I was there, one of the boys had a birthday. His party was simple—he celebrated with a couple of friends and his family. There were chicken wings bought from the grocery store. His dad made sauce from scratch. A cake was obtained. Though their pennies would have to stretch further that month, his parents made every effort to give their son what he wanted.

I was so moved by the genuine love in that home. I carried thoughts of that family with me for the rest of my journey. As I sit and write these words one year after sitting at the table and listening to my friends' troubles, I still feel emotional. They showed me true, pure, whole-hearted love that week.

I can still see their love. It was in the laughter of their children. It was expressed through kisses when they would return home from work. It was felt around the dinner table where they prayed and ate together.

I left their home wondering what kind of example I was creating for the people around me. Was I a motivation to others? Could they see joy amidst my struggles? Or was I allowing my circumstance to define me? Did I radiate love?

Man, that family—they didn't have much money, but they sure had an infinite supply of love.

-GAYLANN AND TRACY-

This story isn't full of glamor. It doesn't have any funny moments. It is not one of those stories that will leave you thinking profound, life-changing thoughts. But, for me, there was something of significant worth taken from the experience. This story is about the day I learned a valuable lesson through the lives of two complete strangers.

I remember meeting them. It was a Sunday. I cannot remember if it was in Louisville or Nashville. I wish I could remember that. On that particular Sunday, I learned that my story really could affect people. I was already aware that it could (and did) impact people in some way, but that day, the effect was deeper and more noticeable. Looking back, I can without a doubt say that I was in the right place at the right time.

The scene was set in the foyer of a church I was attending that particular Sunday. People all around me were talking, finding friends and acquaintances, and drinking coffee. I, however, found myself feeling lonely. I knew no one. There were no familiar faces; no friends to catch up with. As I stood there waiting for the service to start, I began to wonder if I would even have a chance to meet anyone beyond a surface-level smile or handshake. I stood there drinking my coffee, feeling more and more sad. How could all of these people just walk by me and not one of them say a word? This wasn't that big of a church. Couldn't one person say hello to the stranger in the foyer?

It is funny now that I think back on that moment. I expected things from them that I wasn't willing to do myself. I was the one traveling the country sharing my story. I was the one who many times before had initiated conversations. Now, I was the one reluctant to walk up to anyone and share a bit of myself…but that's exactly what I was expecting from them.

I continued to stand there feeling sorry for myself while I drank my coffee and thought cynical thoughts. I began to feel somewhat fed up and angry. I wanted to leave because I selfishly felt like I was wasting my time. It was then that I heard a voice: "Do you go to church here?" I turned to see an older man, likely in his early fifties, inquiring about my presence. "No sir, I do not. I am just passing through because…" I went on to tell him about my adventure. I told him about my cancer. I told him about my hope and I told him of my desire to share that hope with others that I met.

My new friend's name was Gaylann. He sat and listened, grinning from ear to ear. The idea of nomadic wandering all over the map was thrilling to him. He was jealous of my ability to hop in the car and drive, not knowing what would happen next. He told me that he loved my story and the freedom that I possessed. I continued to share the details of my journey and specifically more about my cancer. After some time passed, I felt the mood shift. This man who had been ablaze with enthusiasm now offered up a mere flicker. Gaylann excused himself and I found myself alone again.

I looked around at all of the people still present around me and again wondered why only one person was willing to introduce himself to me. Then suddenly, someone was talking toward me once again. It was Gaylann. This time, he had a woman with him. The woman's name was Tracy, and she was his wife. Gaylann had told her about me, my cancer and my journey, and she wanted to meet me. But she did more than meet me. She opened up to me like I was an old friend. She shared with me about a lump she had recently found. She told me how she had gone to see some doctors and how they were concerned. She said that she would be going in to have the lump removed, and there was a strong possibility that it was cancerous. She had been full of emotion and uncertainty. She had so many reasons to continue living: her husband, children, and grandchildren. Plus her desire to simply live. She wanted to see the Pacific Ocean. She wanted to hike a mountain and smell the strong scent of evergreen trees.

So many things were going through her head as she prepared for something that she wasn't sure she could face. I watched her closely as she shared her fears and uncertainties. I recognized the look in her eyes as the same look I had when I told friends that I had to leave Korea for home. I was not ready to accept the fact that I might have cancer! I couldn't even utter the word. I was not prepared for difficulties of that magnitude.

As I stood across from my new friend, nearly six months after having been diagnosed myself, I knew in that moment that I was so much stronger than I ever realized. I wanted nothing more than to share with her some of the confidence that I had slowly accumulated after hearing of my diagnosis. Fear was visible in her eyes and audible in her words. I wanted to hug her and let her know that everything was going to be all right. Of course, I couldn't remove her burden. I couldn't tell her that she didn't have cancer and I couldn't tell her that there wasn't anything to worry about, but I could tell her that it was okay to be scared. I could let her know that it's okay to not know what you're going to do. Today is today, tomorrow is tomorrow, and yesterday is gone. We cannot change the past. We cannot control the future. We can only appreciate and live for the moments that we find ourselves in. I so badly wanted to inspire her and to motivate her with these words.

As I continued to listen to her talk, I explained that all the emotions she was experiencing and the thoughts she was having were understandable. I also asked that she not let them get the best of her. Having been in Tracy's shoes only months before, I felt confident in my advice. Do not allow any uncertainty to keep you from living life to the fullest. As difficult as it may be, live in the now. If, in a week or two, you find out that you do have cancer, understand this: cancer does *not* define you. You are much more than cancer. You always have been and you always will be.

To be honest, I still don't know the results of Tracy's biopsy. I wish that I did. I thought that I had contact information for Tracy and Gaylann, but I have been unable to find them. I know this though: had I not gone to that particular church, on that particular Sunday, and stood in that particular foyer, I never would have met Gaylann and Tracy. I never would have seen that spark of hope in their eyes as I told them my story. I never would have had the opportunity to point them toward the light at the end of a very long tunnel.

-HANGOVERS, OLD LADIES, AND EASTER SUNDAYS-

Her name was Bo and she was an angel; probably not a real angel, but I imagine a real one would be a lot like her. She was eighty-one years old. Bo had crazy fluffy hair and a high-pitched voice. She was quite frail, maybe standing five foot two. Her kindness and bubbly personality made up for what she lacked in stature. Bo was one of the first people I met after walking in the doors of a church in Asheville, North Carolina.

This particular Sunday happened to be Easter Sunday. My week had been a difficult one. I'd spent a lot of my time wrestling with loneliness, worry, and doubt. The reappearance of an old, bad habit crept up on me as well. I spent Saturday of that week drinking. I drank a lot. I drank because, for whatever reason, I really didn't like myself at that moment in time. The Sunday following my day of inebriation was far from pleasant. The last thing I wanted to do when I woke up was get out of bed. I especially didn't want to go to church. Not only was I physically miserable, but I was feeling guilty. I felt like such a failure for giving in to my old familiar habit.

I resisted for nearly an hour. I remained in the fetal position in my bed of the week, battling whatever it was telling me to get up. I eventually surrendered, despite my fatigue and strong desire to puke.

I managed to shower and head into the city in search of a place of worship. Picking one wasn't difficult—I knew that, no matter where I ended up, I would just be another face in the sea of unfamiliar Easter Sunday churchgoers. I managed to slip into the building without having to talk with many people. I said a few polite hellos, stopped only for a short time by Bo. We exchanged pleasantries and I soon made my way to a seat. My desire to go unnoticed had been mostly successful.

I sat in my seat while others stood and sang. I couldn't help wondering what I was doing there. Yes, I usually attend church on a Sunday, but usually I don't have a hangover. As the people around me sang and clapped, I sat. I felt like a miserable failure. I didn't want to move, let alone stand and sing, but something was pushing me to do just that. The nagging feeling continued, but I resisted...until I looked up and saw her: Bo. This tiny, old woman stood close to the stage, raising her hands and singing. It became obvious that she wasn't bothered by what others around her might be thinking.

Here was a woman with a youthful heart. There was no sign of age or fatigue in her demonstration of worship. She was full of strength and passion. Bo stood out in that audience. She was brightness in a fairly dim room. She was casting light directly into my dark day. I couldn't help but smile watching her.

Bo, nearly three times my age, didn't allow anything to hold her back. My thirty-three-year-old self had no reason to be sitting, brooding. I had no reason to doubt. I had no reason to drown in my guilt. Sure, I had made a mistake, but why allow that mistake to lead to another? That mistake didn't define me. My poor choice would only lead me back to the darkness of my past if I let it. Why not make the choice to get up, move on, and live loud? I took that moment for myself and made a choice. I hit "reset" and pulled myself together. I put the mistakes that I had made behind me. I stood up, sang, and clapped right along with Bo. I knew there would still be stumbling blocks on the path ahead of me, and some would cause me to fall, but I would focus on taking steps *forward*. If Bo can find her joy after eighty-one years on this earth, then so can I.

-THE MORNING OF DEATH-

I avoided writing this story for some time. It's not that I didn't want to write it, but writing it forced me to face a difficult part of my past. Putting the events into words made them feel more real. Writing this story forced me to face the fact that, because of cancer, my friend Preston is now gone.

From my perspective, he didn't "deserve" to die. He was kind and hardworking. His life had been spent serving other people. His death left two children without their father, and one young woman without her husband. He hadn't even reached his thirtieth birthday.

A mutual friend introduced me to Preston. She told me that I really needed to meet him. She told me of many similarities that we had. Honestly, I had no desire to meet him. I had just returned to America.

I had spent the last two years living in Korea. Doctors there told me I had cancer, and sent me home to deal with it. I was convinced my time in the U.S. would be short-lived. I believed that I would be home long enough to have surgery, be un-diagnosed with this cancer they spoke of, and then, back to Korea I would go. I didn't have any time for making new friends. I needed to focus on getting healthy.

Things did not go as I had planned. I learned that I did, in fact, have cancer, and the road to healing would be a long one. At that point in my life, I was attempting to remove myself from a self-imposed dark valley. I had struggled off and on for nearly four years with alcoholism. I had essentially lived for nothing but the next drink. Finding out you have cancer provides a pretty clear opportunity to make a lifestyle change. I attempted to begin a journey down a completely different path, one that didn't include alcoholism. I once again found myself attempting to run toward the faith I had allowed to fall to the wayside.

As I set off toward the path of sobriety, I was reminded again about this Preston person. Preston attended the same Bible college from which I graduated. When I heard this, I was even more apprehensive about meeting him. I wasn't sure I was ready to be around that type of person. Yes, I was seeking the re-establishment of my beliefs, but I also wrestled with the perception of certain "Christians" I had known in the past. I wasn't looking for cheesy or cliché advice at this point in my life.

I was living in Columbia, Missouri, while undergoing treatment. I had graciously been taken in by a family living less than five minutes from the hospital I visited daily for seven weeks. I was, and still am, so thankful for that family. The Messimer family improved my quality of life tenfold. Their kindness and generosity is something that I couldn't possibly put into words. Linda Messimer, the mother of the family, was the one who constantly encouraged me to consider meeting this Preston fellow.

Her sales pitch was something to the effect of: he was married to a Korean woman, and he had spent time teaching English in China. She explained that Preston had also been diagnosed with a rare form of cancer in his neck. She desperately wanted me to know that he and I had a lot in common. She felt strongly that we would connect. After her third or fourth prompting, I finally gave in. I figured we'd meet for coffee and I'd be done with it all.

Preston and I met. He was kind, polite, and definitely knew a few things about Korea. None of this surprised me. In those first minutes of conversation, he seemed to be exactly who I expected him to be. But nothing I told Preston about my past even made him flinch. I was open and honest, and he listened without judgment. Something about him seemed different. As he dropped me off at the Messimers' house, I casually informed him of my upcoming trip to St. Louis to visit a friend. We exchanged farewells, and he gave me his phone number. He told me to call if I ever needed anything. To be honest, I didn't think I'd ever see him again. I had enjoyed our time together, but I wasn't sure I was ready for that much "goodness" in my life. I was relearning a life lived for Jesus, and I wanted to take it slow.

Later that week, I was approached by Linda. She handed me an envelope that had been left in her office. It had been left by Preston, who I learned helped my host family with campus ministry at the University of Missouri. *Of course he does*, I thought. *That guy is a freaking saint!* I opened the envelope and found a note: "I don't know if you believe in little birdies, but one told me you might be headed to St. Louis. I hope this helps." Along with the note was a $100 bill. I was shocked by this generous gift, but more shocked by a revelation: He had listened to every word I said, and sought a way to encourage me.

My trip to St. Louis had been a trivial detail when you considered all that Preston and I had talked about. We spoke of our dealings with cancer and my struggles with alcohol. He listened beyond that, and he recognized an opportunity to bless me in a way I didn't deserve. I was deeply touched.

About a week later, I was in desperate need of a ride. I didn't have a car, and was currently in no condition to drive anyway. I called a couple of my friends, but they were unable to help. I understood they all had jobs and obligations, but I did not know how I was going to get things done. Then I remembered Preston's offer. So...I called him. He headed my way without hesitation. He took me where I needed to go, and we even hung out a bit afterward.

Soon after that day, Preston and I met for a meal of Korean food. Next, he had me over to his home where I met his wife and kids. He became a part of my life, and I was a part of his. I had grown to love my new friend.

Not long after our relationship began to form, it was time for me to begin my Coffee with Cooper journey. Before I left, I shared my hopes and concerns with Preston. He knew I sought to improve my life. He was aware of my desire to cling to faith and leave drunkenness behind. I asked him to pray for me, and he was willing. He told me to call whenever I felt the need.

Within three weeks of my journey's beginning, I learned that Preston had gotten very sick. He was on a rough road on a downward slope. Hospice care became necessary. I attempted to call him, but he was usually too tired or ill from medication to speak. Sometimes the phone would ring until voicemail picked up, but from time to time I would speak with his brother. He did his best to keep me informed, but I missed my friend.

I continued on my way, doing my best to stay the course. At some point, I felt this invisible pull to be honest with Preston about my current state. I knew he probably wouldn't be able to talk, but I decided to call. To my surprise, he answered. I was caught off guard, and found myself lost for words. He asked how I was doing, and how my trip was going. I did my best to fill him in quickly (I could tell he was tired) and let him know about some of the struggles I had been having with trying not to drink too much. I told him that I wanted to do and be better. I apologized for the time and prayers he had wasted on me. Preston was quick to let me know that his time had not been wasted. He said that my "bad choices" didn't define me unless I allowed them to. He let me know that he was proud of the journey I was taking, and for my attempts to change. I wanted to talk more, but I could sense that my friend was having a difficult time communicating. The last words he said were "I love you." I let him know I loved him, too, and hung up the phone.

I wish I had realized at the time how precious that moment was, but I allowed myself to get caught up in life once again. It wasn't until a few weeks after that phone call that I remembered the need to pray for Preston. I had heard he wasn't doing well and that things were looking really bad. I sat in my quiet room and I prayed: *God, so many people love Preston. We want him here with us, but more than anything, we don't want him to suffer. Give*

Preston peace. Take away his pain. I pray for Your will to be done. Do what needs to be done in the life of my friend, Preston.

The next morning I woke to the news that Preston had passed away. My heart dropped. This was not what I wanted. Why, God? Why him? I lay in bed and cried. I thought of his wife and children. I thought of his parents and siblings. I thought of every life he had ever touched, including mine. The tears continued to flow.

I wrestled with "why" for the next week. I prayed a lot, pleading with God to explain. The longer I wondered, and the more I prayed, the more clear it became. Preston's life was so short, but he had used his time so wisely. He had become a light in an ever-darkening world. In the short time we had together, he shone brightly into the darkness that encompassed my life. Despite his dealings with a deadly disease, he went out of his way to help me with my struggles. He put his own needs and desires aside, and placed mine in a position of importance. If he had done this for me in such a short time of being friends, I can only imagine what he did in the lives of those he had known longer.

-COCAINE VS. CANCER-

I was sitting in a room full of people that I had only just met. My host for the week in Baltimore was one of those people. I had connected with him through a mutual friend, and he had welcomed me into his home for the week. Not knowing anyone had me feeling slightly uneasy about sharing my story. Would they really have an interest in hearing about my battle with cancer?

I don't know why I was struggling with insecurity. I had already traveled a few thousand miles. My story had successfully been shared a number of times along the way. I had experienced intimate moments with former strangers. There had been positive responses to my thoughts of the past and dreams for the future. So why was I reluctant now?

Why did I feel like this instance was any different than the others? The only real difference was the location. Despite my reluctance, I decided to share my story. I talked about my life before cancer, and the crooked path my life had taken. I told of my diagnosis and treatment. I verbally led them down the path that carried me to that very home in Baltimore. In response, the room of strangers did act as if they were interested. I still felt uneasy, but continued until the final sentence of the story left my lips.

I was surprised when one man spoke up very quickly. He was older than most of the people in the group, though still young. He looked into my eyes intently and said, "Your story just blows my mind. It is so powerful!" His words made me smile. "You are an inspiration. You were given a 5% chance of survival, and here you are making the choice to be positive." I am certain that I blushed as I expressed my thanks.

He continued to speak, sharing with me his own story. He told me that he had used cocaine every day for over ten years. On top of drug addiction, he also struggled with alcoholism. Along his own crooked path, my new friend had been introduced to Jesus. He overcame the obstacles in his life by surrendering everything to Christ. It had not been an easy choice, and each day had its challenges, but he found more joy now than at any other time in his life.

His jagged, rocky road had led him somewhere amazing, yet he still found inspiration in my story. I found this shocking. In my eyes, his story was far more powerful than mine could ever be. He disagreed, saying that I had looked death in the eye and turned my life around. It was an amazing moment that I won't ever forget.

I was so thankful that we had probably not-so-randomly ended up in the same room in Baltimore that evening. I was also thankful that I found the mental strength to share my story once again. This former stranger and I had a mutual appreciation for where we had each been, and how far we had come. We had both entered that home feeling different and maybe a little uncomfortable, but would leave feeling encouraged and motivated to carry on.

And carry on I did.

-DON'T JUDGE STRIPPERS BY THEIR TITLE-

I used to think that nothing could beat a good beer and a hot meal, but throw a couple of strippers into the mix and you've got yourself an unforgettable affair. When I was in Baltimore, I had the privilege of experiencing all of these things "at the same time" (a little *Office Space* humor for any fans out there). Let me just tell you right off the bat: It. Was. Life. Changing. I had never actually seen a stripper in my life, let alone talked to one. When presented with the opportunity to do just that, I could not pass it up. There were two of them. They both came to my table and sat with me. They were beautiful, extremely beautiful. To be honest...I was very nervous at first. I felt intimidated in their presence. I mean, *they were strippers!* As they both sat there with me, I was overtaken by their charm. They were smiling, laughing at my jokes, and showing genuine interest in our conversation. I could not help but completely enjoy the time I was having with them! It was just me, my host for the week, and two strippers! Could it really get any better?

Actually, it could. The place where we had gathered was a cool, local pub. A hotspot, nonetheless. Our basis for choosing this fine establishment for the evening? The Monday night special. It was a big meal, designed for a hungry man, at a very reasonable price. It included generously sized pieces of chicken alongside an even more generously sized portion of mashed potatoes. I was impressed. It was delicious. I also appreciated the atmosphere that made up this hometown hotspot. In the background, you could hear people singing karaoke. Not everyone who sang on that Monday night was in line to be the next American Idol, but that made it even more enjoyable. I liked that a majority of the people were not the best singers. I was glad that people felt like they could passionately sing their heart out on this stage without fear of judgment by the other people in the room. It was like a giant room full of friends, and I was sitting with the best of them.

As we sat there eating, I was sharing my story and also hearing some of theirs. To put it simply, I was moved by their stories. Some of the most wonderful words from my entire journey were uttered while sitting in that pub with a pair of strippers. They were so genuine in character and had truly beautiful souls. Both had experienced a series of difficulties in the past, as a result of what they would call "bad choices," but now, they spoke passionately of their strivings to be different. They had chosen to wholeheartedly run in a completely different direction. They were the first to admit that they were far from perfect, but their desire for a different life was real and encouraging.

I had a few encounters with them during my stay in Baltimore. The two of them could easily be found hanging out together considering they were very close friends. I guess you could say that I was one of their "regulars" by the end of the week. Each time, I was excited to hear more about their lives. I enjoyed listening to them as they talked about how they used to live, and how much different things were now. Their words seemed to fuel my passion for my own journey. And at the same time, their journey made mine seem so...trivial. Suddenly cancer seemed so small. My time with them was a mere pit stop. I knew that it wouldn't last long, so I did my best to embrace every moment that I could. I soaked up every bit of motivation that those two strippers had to offer.

When I think back to my first night at the pub, I often find myself thinking about those karaoke singers. Even if they were awful, they each gave it their all. They did not let anything hold them back. They fearlessly stood on that stage and passionately delivered their message. And then there were the two former strippers that I met. These two *men* (what were you thinking here, people? Get your mind out of the gutter!) who I had the privilege of getting to know were now living their lives in the same way that the karaoke rock stars were living theirs: with passion, not tainted by those around them.

My stripper friends now find themselves standing on a different stage, singing a different tune. They know there will be people who look at their past and completely dismiss them. They know that others will likely fail to understand why they left stripping to pursue their faith. These men, who once stood on stage in their birthday suits, are standing up for something completely different now: their conviction.

There are two things that come to mind as I reach the conclusion of this story. The first is this: throughout this story, I crafted my words in a way that I wanted my readers to assume I was implying certain things, when really I wasn't. There are two types of people that may have been offended as I attempted to do such:

1. The person who does not think it is funny to insinuate anything about this subject matter *and*

2. Any person who may have been or still is a stripper. To those in category number one, please, get over yourself. To those of you in category number two, it was not (nor ever will be) my intention to mock your current or your past profession.

I sincerely apologize if I came off as insensitive. And while I may not be available to come and watch you perform, I am always willing to sit down, have a fried chicken dinner, rock out to some karaoke, and hear your story.

I wonder how often we critique those around us based on a single glimpse at their life. How many of you gasped when I said, "I hung out with strippers"? How many of you questioned my behavior or possibly my journey as a whole? How often do we presume to know the entire story before we actually take the time to finish hearing it?

"Try to understand men. If you understand each other, you will be kind to each other. Knowing a man well never leads to hate and almost always leads to love." -John Steinbeck

-THE MAN THEY CALL FRANK-

Who is this man they call Frank? I honestly don't know him at all, but he seems to be someone that a lot of people hold in high regard.

As I sat in a cafe (one that I would consider a hidden gem in downtown Baltimore), I was surprised that it was so empty. People were clearly missing out. I spoke with the barista as he made my drink. He was a nice guy. He had lived in Baltimore for most of his life. We talked about coffee and the art of making drinks. He told me of his opportunities to travel some, but not as much as he would like. He spoke of the time he had taken a month-long trip to China. Having spent time in Korea, his trip sparked my interest. We spoke about the different parts of Asia and the culture there. It was a nice conversation.

I finished my second Americano and was about to leave, when a fairly large group of people walked in. I took my time gathering my things, giving myself time to observe the group. They were intriguing, obviously locals, and I hoped for the opportunity to start up a conversation. One of them looked my way, and acknowledged my shirt! It was a black tee with a picture of a humerus bone on the front, along with the phrase "I found this humerus" (haha, get it?).

The group began to have an intense conversation about a man they called Frank. I felt like I was in a movie. You know the scene: somewhere in the heart of a big city, where a group of well-dressed locals enter their hangout (stage left). Speaking with a thick, Baltimore accent: "Ehhh, where's Frank? Yo!! Bah bee!!! (That's Bobby in "Baltimorese," obviously) Where is Frank?? Ehhh, I mean, I heard he was here, but he's not! I hope he is okay..."

As I continued to prepare for my own exit, I listened as the scene played out. I learned that they all had a friend named Frank, whom they genuinely cared for. They seemed to be concerned about his wellbeing. Another member of the group spoke up with information that the others didn't seem to have: Frank had been in an accident and the odds were not in his favor.

I don't know Frank, but in that moment I learned something about him. As he lives his life, Frank is leaving a mark. It's not just any old mark, but a large and positive impression. Frank, who was not even present, had influenced this group of friends in such a way that they were using their time to express their love and concern for him. No one was gossiping about Frank or talking about bad choices that he may (or may not) have made. Frank had influenced these people in such a way that, even in his absence, they were giving him positive attention. His impression on this group of people was nothing but good.

This got me thinking: What would a group of people have to say about me if I were in Frank's position? What would be said about me if I was unable to make it to our regular spot for the daily cup of Joe? Would they even notice my absence? Would they be worried? Concerned? What would they say?! And when they spoke of me, would their conversation attract the attention of passersby? Would it leave them with a desire to know more about me?

-JONAH IN THE WHALE-

It had been nearly seven years since I had seen Heather. When I got a message stating she was living in Baltimore and wanted to meet up for lunch and coffee, I was thrilled. I looked forward to the opportunity to reunite with a dear friend *and* meet her son. Before our meeting, she warned me that she was as pregnant as she could possibly be. I took her warning in stride and prepared for our afternoon together.

Upon arrival, I spotted my very pregnant friend. Her belly was beautiful and full of life. She was an adorable pregnant girl. Her walk alone, though likely painful, was enough to melt the hardest of hearts. During lunch she joked that her son, who was to be named Jonah, could possibly arrive at any moment. His due date had come and gone. She said, "If he says it's time, then it's time!" As great of a story as it would have made, she did not go into labor that day. Regardless of his late arrival, Jonah would play a rather significant role in my stay in Baltimore.

Lunch with my long-lost friend was wonderful. Our conversations contained many stories, allowing us to catch up and reminisce. Afterward, my very pregnant friend and

I hugged and parted ways. I didn't know it at the time, but we would meet again much sooner than planned.

I continued on with my week in fairly normal fashion. One particular day greeted me with heavy cloud cover. I had gotten off to a much later start than anticipated. A late start usually didn't bother me—I was never really on a set schedule—but on this day I had wanted an earlier start. I was hoping to have coffee with the morning crowd rather than the afternoon and evening ones I had grown familiar with.

When I finally started my car and headed into the city, I noticed a little red light on the dashboard. It was a little red battery. I assumed it was a little low on charge, and I'd be fine as long as I kept my jumper cables close.

There are some really sweet coffee shops in Baltimore. If you have never been to "The Greatest City in America" you should check it out. Even if you are not into coffee, downtown Baltimore is just full of rich culture and beautiful history.

I enjoyed a long day of Americanos and good conversation. As evening approached, I decided to return to the home of the man who was hosting me that week. Unlike most other weeks on my journey, I was staying with a person I didn't know from Adam. After our week together, I consider him a dear friend, but when I first arrived at his home, he was a complete stranger. We were put in touch with each other by a mutual friend, who had asked if he would consider hosting me during my time in Baltimore. I will be forever grateful that he said yes.

On the way to my host's house, it started to pour rain. It was raining so hard that even with the windshield wipers on it was difficult to see anything in front of you. As I drove, I leaned forward to try to make sense of the road ahead of me. Out of nowhere, my car stopped running. It just stopped. Thankfully, I was able to make my way to the side of the road without any issues. I had come to a halt in front of a car lot. Of course. I attempted to restart my car and was greeted with the sound of silence. Nothing was working.

I am certain that if I had asked my host Billy for his help, he would have done anything within his power to assist me; but there was something about reaching out to anyone (let alone a stranger) as I faced this obstacle that just didn't feel appropriate. I racked my brain for a solution (and tried to start my car over and over again) and felt that my only real option was to call AAA. They told me it would be nearly an hour before they arrived, so I sat and waited. I pondered what would happen next. How was I going to afford a new battery? My budget was so tight. Too tight, I realized. Why hadn't I prepared for moments like this?

I sat there feeling angry and stupid. I sat in the pouring rain, only protected by my useless car. I decided to try starting my car for the hundredth time. To my utter shock, it started. I thought fast, throwing it into gear and hitting the gas as hard as I could. I wasn't going to sit and wait for AAA, I was going to try to get to Billy's house as fast as possible. So, on I drove. I hit green light after green light. I was convinced that I would make it. I was so close, until that single, stupid red light. I sat there, sweating bullets, praying that engine would continue to purr. The rain poured, the wind blew, the light turned green...and my car died.

This day had quickly turned into one of the worst on my journey, by far. My car was dead. The light was green and cars behind me were honking, unaware of my current state of affairs. I couldn't turn on my hazard lights. Rolling down the electric windows to wave them on was not an option. I opened my door in an attempt to signal the cars behind me, but the monsoon outside forced me back inside.

Cars flew by me as I sat, unmoving, at the intersection. I was clearly enjoying sitting in the rain and stalling all traffic, so horns continued to blare. After what felt like an eternity (but likely was three to five minutes) I decided I would have to get out and push. I forced my door open, put the car in neutral, and put my feet on the road. I moved the car a distance greater than my junior-high boy figure should have been capable of, and managed to get to the side of the road. I climbed back inside, soaked, angry, and unaware of my next move. I decided to call AAA again and informed them of my current location.

I still had no idea what I was going to do when they did come to help me. I had a limited budget and extremely limited options. While I waited, I googled my problems. As it sometimes does, this only made things worse. Some of the suggestions were even more overwhelming than simply replacing the battery (as if that thought hadn't been overwhelming enough). My problem may be the alternator. Great. I felt like I had the weight of the world on my shoulders. All I really wanted to do was cry, but I decided to call my sweet, pregnant friend Heather instead. She's one of those rational people, always ready with a sensible solution. She also offers a great amount of comfort and peace in difficult moments. I let her know what was going on, and she immediately offered to meet me and give me a ride to wherever I needed to be. Without hesitation, Heather loaded her toddler and immensely pregnant self into her SUV and headed my way. When she arrived, she hopped out of her car into the pouring rain and waddled over to me, telling me to wait for AAA in her car. She was effortlessly able to calm me down, reassuring me that everything would be just fine. My friend also let me know that her husband happens to be a "car guy." As we sat, she called her husband to see what he thought. She listed the symptoms and received an unfavorable diagnosis: he thought it was the alternator.

There I was, on the east coast of the United States, 850 miles from home. I was staring out the window at my hunk-of-junk car as the rain poured down. The money in my wallet would not get me far. I was stranded.

I quietly hoped my stress would not transfer to my friend, sending her into impending labor. Thankfully, Jonah stayed put and AAA finally arrived. The driver, my friend, and I discussed my options, and we concluded leaving the car in the Sears parking lot would be best for now. Their large parking lot and auto shop offered the safest solution.

I was nervous about the unknown events of the next day, but my friend and her charming smile put me at ease. Kindness was her natural reaction, and I was thankful. She gave me a ride back to my host home and told me I could count on her for a ride the next morning as well. I was still fearful of what was to come, but I found great comfort in her presence.

The next day, my overdue friend showed up right on time. She looked so joyful, especially for a person in her current state. I was so thankful to Jonah for his delayed arrival. He seemed to be inheriting his mother's spirit of kindness.

Sears agreed to look over the car and give me an official diagnosis and estimate before they did any work. We knew it would be a while, so we headed to my friend's house and waited. Sears finally called and gave us the news: I needed a new alternator, and it would cost me $380. I felt sick. Considering my financial status, $380 was a big deal. My nightmarish thoughts were suddenly interrupted: "Cooper, I talked to Eric and we want to help you." My friend told me that they would be willing to loan me the money to fix my car, and would allow me to pay them back whenever I could. I couldn't even believe it. I was overwhelmed with gratitude.

Long story short, the alternator was fixed and paid for. Soon, following that horrible, cloudy day, I was able to pay my friend back. Regardless of my fears in those difficult moments, everything worked out. I am forever grateful to my friend and her family for sacrificing financially for me. And I am thankful to Jonah for delaying his arrival and making it all possible. He stayed in the belly of his mama until my problems were sorted out. If he had arrived on time, there is no telling what would have happened to me and my journey.

-NEWTON VS. WEST NEWTON-

The weather could not have been more perfect: eighty degrees and a bright, blue sky. There was nothing but the road ahead of me. I was so excited. Soon, I would reunite with two friends I hadn't seen in far too long. I would be spending a week with them and experiencing life in Pittsburgh.

I was especially pleased on this particular drive because I had awakened early and departed as the sun was rising. My early departure meant that when I arrived at my friend's home, the sun would still be up! The travels to my previous destinations usually ended with me arriving in the dark hours of the night. The cause of these late arrivals was usually a good one: I often had lunch with my host family of the previous week before taking off toward my next adventure. It was always nice to have one last encounter with those who had invested an entire week of their time in me.

On this particular week, I was leaving the city of Baltimore. I had an amazing time in "Charm City" but, much like the conclusion of trips to other cities, I was ready to take on the next. My journey was now taking me to a small town just outside of Pittsburgh. I had never been to Pittsburgh, and was excited for the opportunity to visit.

The town awaiting my arrival was West Newton. I set my GPS by entering in the address given to me by my soon-to-be host family. For reasons unknown to me at the time, my faithful GPS was having trouble finding the street where they lived. I figured that the lack of updating on my navigation system was hindering its locating abilities, but I wasn't too worried; it hadn't failed me yet. Not wanting to waste any time, I entered what I felt to be the most common street name I could think of (Main Street) and my soon-to-be city of the week, "Newton, Pennsylvania." Upon my arrival, I intended to call my friend and have him navigate me the rest of the way to his home.

Nearly four hundred miles. Six and a half hours. I was right on schedule to arrive in time for dinner. When my GPS informed me that I was a little over an hour away, I decided to stop for some fuel, and a moment to give my host family a call. I practically skipped around the gas station, making very little effort to conceal my joy and excitement. I remember being so thankful and even expressing that thanks toward God. I was just... So. Happy.

I made my way back to the car and decided to pull up the address of my destination on my phone. This method of navigation was more up-to-date and accurate, but I used my faithful GPS the majority of the time in an attempt to save data. Since I was getting fairly close, I decided that I would use my phone's navigation system the rest of the way. I entered the street name and number and asked my phone to lead me the rest of the way. To my surprise, the phone projected a three hundred mile trek in my future. Whaaaaaaaaaaaaat?

I consulted my GPS, which still said I was only a little over an hour away. I looked back at my phone and re-entered the given address. Again, my search resulted in a three hundred mile drive to the destination.

Whaaaaa? I just drove more than three hundred of my nearly four hundred projected miles! How could I have three hundred to go?

I decided to call my host and ask his advice. He asked me where I was. I chuckled and said, "I'm almost to Newton." He replied, "West Newton, right?" I thought, *What does it matter as long as I'm in Newton?* He repeated, "You're headed for West Newton, right?" It was then that I had one of those face-palm moments and I realized why I couldn't find the street address in the GPS: it really didn't exist.

The distance from my previous destination to West Newton: roughly four hundred miles. The distance from my previous destination to plain old Newton: roughly four hundred miles. The distance between West Newton and plain old Newton: three hundred miles. I had driven toward the wrong Newton for six hours.

Immediately, f-bomb after f-bomb after f-bomb spilled from my mouth. I had made a horrible mistake. I had driven in the wrong direction. I hit the steering wheel nearly a dozen times, allowing the f-bomb to continue to flow freely.

In that moment, a verse from the Book of James came to my mind. The one where he speaks of the tongue and how we use it to praise God one minute and curse Him the next. Sure, that's exactly what was happening, but I was so not in the mood for Bible verses. *God, this is not the time!* I thought to myself. I thought I was so close, but I had actually *driven to the wrong side of the state!* My frustration got the best of me, and I continued to swear loudly. It was satisfying to scream those words of contempt. I won't lie. It really, really was.

After my tantrum, I paused, and had another thought. I found myself thinking that, if one of my closest friends was in this situation, I would find it easy to laugh at such a silly mistake. So, why couldn't I laugh about this? I didn't feel like laughing, mainly because it was my silly mistake, but I tried.

I pushed out fake laugh after fake laugh. I forced choked chuckles until my laughter became real. I called a friend I knew would laugh with me, and told him of my blunder. He didn't disappoint. At my expense, he laughed, which only made me laugh harder.

I knew I couldn't change what had happened. It had been done (or, driven) and it couldn't be taken back. The miles were behind me. The fuel was spent. Daylight was fading. My one and only choice was to drive on!

With another three hundred miles ahead, I had time to ponder. Life is a lot like my West Newton vs. Newton encounter. One moment you think you're headed in the "right" direction, when suddenly you're pushed in another. Plans are made to do specific things, and those plans are interrupted by things that were previously unknown.

Living with cancer comes with a lot of unknowns. Cancer itself was my wake-up call. I had been on the path I thought I was supposed to be heading down when a tumor came along and showed me I had been traveling in the wrong direction the whole time. It took a lot of time for me to deal with that—longer than the minutes spent taking out my frustration on a steering wheel. I still deal with anger of some level from time to time. Though, in many ways, I am thankful for my new direction. This new path has taken me so many amazing places and taught me innumerable lessons.

-TKO'd BY A
THREE-YEAR-OLD-

S omewhere around the ninth week of my journey, I felt like I had grown accustomed to the flow with which it was progressing. I had already spent eight weeks on eight different couches. I had ventured around eight cities, swum through a sea of faces, and experienced a wide collection of coffeehouses. A variety of conversations had occurred, during which I shared my story and my reasons for traveling. I had my game face and a speech to go with it: "Hello. I am Cooper. I am in your city as part of a journey across the country. I am fighting 'incurable' cancer." I had no fear. I had it all figured out. I would even joke about my cancer on occasion. I made reference to myself as (read this in your best TV announcer voice) "Cancer Boy: spreading hope amongst the masses." I was looking into the face of cancer and screaming, "No! I will not be defined by you!" And if I could be strong in the midst of something so difficult, then so could they!

This likeness of myself was presented with complete sincerity, but at times it may have been a little stronger than I was actually feeling. As I stood outside of the home where I would spend my week in Pittsburgh, I began to soak in my surroundings. I heard one of my hosts, the mother of a three-year-old girl, speaking to her daughter. She instructed young Madison to hold her hand as we all crossed the street together. I don't know why it happened. I had been there such a short time and barely even spoken to the child, and I had definitely not offered her my protective services, but she grabbed my hand instead of her mother's. I don't know why, but something about her naive act made me feel as though I was crumbling, breaking apart from the inside out.

Later that evening, I was lying on the couch watching a baseball game and spending some time writing. Madison walked up to me and asked me what I was doing. I told her, and she proceeded to just crawl up next to me. She silently watched the game, as I did the same. She didn't ask questions or even talk, she just watched the game, and watched me as I watched the game.

I don't know why, but again, I felt myself crumbling.

She continued to watch this game with me into the evening, rarely interrupting. I began to feel drowsy after a long day full of driving, so I informed my little friend that I was ready to go to sleep. I remember her turning to me, with her bright blue eyes in the lead. She placed her head to my chest and acted as though she was sleeping. Her little, fake snore rattled on as she pressed her head against me.

I felt myself continue to crumble.

The next day, I was able to have coffee with my host and a friend of their family. Madison joined us with her morning cereal. As we sat there talking, she attempted multiple times to engage in conversation. She wanted to talk to me. She wanted my attention. Her mother noted that this was unusual, that Madison was far from open with people she didn't know well. In fact, she was just plain shy. She was known to stick to her parents' sides. For some reason, this was not the case with me.

She continued to vie for my attention. Her mother asked her to, "Please be quiet while Mommy and Cooper talk," and told her that she would get her chance a little later. I could not help but smile, feeling a little special. I felt as though I could melt.

On the same day, I began to notice some things happening with my body that did not feel quite normal. I started having some symptoms that gave me pause. I wondered if I should call my doctor, but I feared hearing the words, "We need you to come home." If I went home, I would miss out on my allotted time in Pittsburgh, and possibly other cities. If I went home, I would have to step off the scheduled path of Coffee with Cooper! There was no way I was letting that happen, so I ignored the problem and went on with my day.

I was very productive. I ventured into the city and hit up a local dive diner. I had some awful coffee and downed some okay food. I drove a family friend to the train station and ran some other errands. And then…I began to notice those symptoms coming back. There was a tightness in the side of my neck and some numbness in my face. I also had a choking feeling in my throat and tingling in the back of the neck along my spinal chord. I knew very well that I had recently had ten pounds of tumor removed from my neck and that I had just completed weeks of radiation treatment. I desperately hoped that this was only my body responding to all of the trauma it had endured, but I didn't have the assurance of absolute truth, as a companion by my side.

I should have called the doctor right away, but the thought of having to quit my trip was overwhelming. What if I found out that I was dying? Both possibilities troubled me. Despite the fact that I had been so tough when I shared my story many times before, I was scared. I had laughed at the idea of death, or claimed to have accepted the possibility it would come soon; but now I was shaking in my skinny jeans.

I decided that at least giving my nurses a call would be a good idea. I would give them the heads up, and let them know what exactly I was dealing with. I would keep them informed, but let them know that I was *not* going to quit my adventure. Despite the fear, I felt willing to die doing what was making me the happiest I had been in a very long time.

I made the phone call to the nurses. I was informed that they would talk to my doctor and call me back. Waiting for that call was difficult. Honestly, it felt like Hell. Thankfully, I had a little gem named Madison to distract me. She was simply doing what most of the other children her age were doing…playing. She desperately wanted to involve me in her playtime. She loved to be picked up, twirled, and hugged. She was so sweet. And with each giggle she emitted, I melted.

Between the pings of sweet laughter, I heard my phone ringing. I had to take a large step outside of the world that was distracting me from my reality. I walked into the hallway, toward the silence so that I could hear the words that I did not want to hear. "We need you to come home." They said that they wanted to take a closer look at some of the things that I was dealing with. They were not worried about some of my symptoms, but the numbness to the face was a concern. My mind was screaming, "*No!*" but my lips slowly said, "Okay. I understand. I will be there in a couple of days." And with that, I hung up.

I stood alone for a few moments, taking it all in. I wondered how I could get so far into this journey and now have to give up. Why was this happening? I was not even halfway done and I had no desire to stop. I was being taken out of the game. I knew that I could bring home the trophy, but now I felt like I was being cut from the team.

I found my host, and explained to her what the nurses had informed me. She was more than supportive, though saddened that I would have to leave. I only made it three days into my week in Pittsburgh before being pulled away. If this were not enough, my newest sidekick had been looking forward to our continued playtime. Having to explain to my tiny little friend that I had to leave, and hearing her ask when I'd be back, was heart-wrenching. I simply didn't have the strength to answer.

My host informed me that she wanted to fill my gas tank before I made the cross-country drive back to central Missouri, and I gratefully accepted her offer. When we arrived at the gas station, I attempted to prepare myself for the uncertainties ahead of me. I was pulled from my thoughts when I heard Madison calling for me from inside her mother's van. I approached her side of the car, peeked in, and said, "Hi!" She smiled, and asked if we could go home and play. Madison's mom did her best to explain that I had to leave, but that I might come back soon. She asked Madison if she wanted a hug from Cooper. She quickly said, "Yes!" so I climbed into the back of the van and unhooked her from her car seat. I scooped her up and gave her a silly look. She looked back, smiling and laughing. I smiled and laughed, too, though I was feeling so full of fear. Then she hugged me as tight as her little arms could. She looked back at me and smiled again. I barely held myself together as I placed her back into her car seat and buckled her in. I smiled at her one more time as I waved goodbye.

I headed back toward my car when Madison's mom called out to me once more. "Wait! Madison got you something." She rummaged through her purse, eventually pulling out a keychain. It was a small pod with two peas in it, with an attached sign reading, "two peas in a pod." I have to be honest and say that I am not a fan of random keychains, but just then, I felt as though I had won the lottery. I knew that I needed to thank my little friend, and get in one more goodbye. I could feel the surge of emotions about to surface, so I knew that I needed to make it fast.

As I drove down the highway in my car, my face drenched in tears, I tried to understand my emotions. I was feeling fearful. I had been putting my fears on the backburner for the last nine weeks of my journey. I acknowledged it occasionally, but I usually sort of laughed it off. I knew that my reason for fear was real, and even appropriate, especially considering my current state. The other emotions had been caused by a little girl named Madison. Her tiny gift made me feel something that I could not even attempt to explain. She had filled me with a joy that

I cannot put into words. She had knocked me to the ground with her relentless, childlike love.

I continued to cry as I drove and to drive as I cried. I'm certain that I looked like a fool, but I didn't care, I just continued to sob...until I reached home.

-IT WASN'T ME!
OKAY, IT WAS-

I am quite confident in saying, as a little boy, I was a living nightmare. My intense energy drove my mom crazy. I spent my days running around the house, swinging off of the kitchen cabinets like a little monkey. I was also ornery. I did a lot of disobeying and mouthing. My mom told me later in my adult life that she had to beg God for strength on a daily basis. I was a little terror.

Getting away with these things with Mom was an easy task. Getting away with things with Dad was a completely different story. Actually, it was an impossible task. As a child, my dad terrified me. He wasn't mean, but he firmly disciplined me for my behavior.

The second I heard Dad walk through the door after a day at work, I had an uncomfortable feeling in my gut. Hearing his work boots echo their pound off the floor, I knew I was in for a reprimand for my behavior earlier that day. I did what any little boy would do, and ran and hid under my sister's bed. Thankfully, I've grown out of my bad behavior. At thirty-three years of age, even in the moments where I slip up, I certainly do not see a need for my father to discipline me.

These memories of my childhood came to mind when my journey took me to Chicago. I knew my friend and host for the week, Candy, from a summer spent teaching English in Bosnia. It had been ten years since we had seen each other, so I was thrilled to be seeing her again. We had so much catching up to do, and so many memories to reminisce. Oh, and I finally got to meet her giant of a husband, as well as their children.

One of the hardest things about Coffee with Cooper was moving from house to house week after week. It was sometimes awkward starting over and introducing myself to a new family. I didn't really mind, but many times I was showing up at a house where I knew one spouse and hadn't yet met the other. Often, my hosts were girls I'd known from past adventures. Now, I know what you're thinking, but it wasn't like that. I have always been "mom guy." I was always closer to my mom. I have always connected well with friends' moms. I tend to connect more easily with girls in general. Like I said... I'm a mom guy.

Though I knew our relationships were purely platonic, I tried to visualize things from the perspective of the men in their respective lives. Here I was, random guy in his mid-thirties showing up at their house. I would be sleeping on their couch or in their spare room, hanging out in their space while they were at work and eating some of their food. I can only imagine how strange it was for some of those men who were meeting me for the very first time. I can honestly say that every one of my hosts was gracious and kind and these imaginings occurred only in my mind...but I do wonder what some of them were thinking.

My first morning in Chicago got off to a slow start. No one else was home when I started my morning with cereal and coffee. I didn't mind. I enjoyed the solitude. My plan for the day was to explore Chicago, but I knew I needed to shower after my previous day of driving. I headed to the bathroom to clean up. I also decided to search for some Tylenol because I had woken up with a horrible headache. My hosts' bathroom had a cabinet that sat behind their toilet. It had two glass doors that opened to provide access to the shelves inside. On one shelf of the cabinet sat a cool, antique medicine bottle. I decided to look inside, thinking that maybe they still stored medicine inside. I went to open the cabinet doors, but had some trouble. I had to tug a bit harder than I thought I should for the door to release. As I tugged, a pretty glass figurine left its perch atop the cabinet. I felt pretty bad for breaking this collectible piece, and bent down to clean up the shards of glass. In the process, I noticed something that made my stomach flip: there was a chunk of material missing *from the toilet*. In falling, the figurine took a two-to three-inch chunk of the porcelain throne along with it. I frantically looked for the missing piece while trying to figure out what the heck I was going to do.

The glass on the floor became strewn pieces of a puzzle, and I had to find the right one. I spotted "the one" and grabbed it from the mess. I attempted to put it back in its place, thinking that I could just find some sort of glue or putty and fix it. Surely that would solve everything! I held the piece there, convincing myself that everything was going to be okay. I tried flushing the toilet to prove to myself that this would be an easy fix. I quickly realized that I was wrong. So wrong. Water began to spray all over the bathroom floor. At that moment, I heard the front door open and large feet echoing across the floor. Dad was home, and I was about to get it.

"Hello?" Candy's husband's voice called from the kitchen. He was a guy's guy. Tall with wide shoulders and a deep voice. I wear skinny jeans and size small flannel. Upon our meeting, Candy's husband had instantly gained my respect. Knowing that I couldn't hide, I stepped out of the bathroom. I explained what had happened and led him to the bathroom. There was my pride all over the bathroom floor, a pile of glass and toilet water. He took one look at my mistake and said, "Well, looks like I am going to get a new toilet." I wanted to offer right then and there to replace the toilet with my own money, but I knew that my budget wouldn't allow it.

My friend's husband was kind. He knew what my journey was about and told me that I could go about my business and he would take care of my mistake. As tempting as that sounded, I knew that I couldn't do that. Even though I knew I could not pay, I offered to go to Lowe's with him. It was so awkward for me. I felt shame. I felt stupid. I felt like a failure all around.

While we were at Lowe's, my host picked up a new toilet and the supplies needed to install it. He also picked up some random provisions for other projects around his house. We headed back with the new toilet, and I wanted nothing more than to help him install it. In a bathroom made for one, there wasn't room for two to work, so I stood by the door and offered my assistance whenever possible.

When the job was complete and the bathroom was once again clean, I felt that it would be safe for me to head out for the rest of the day. I did not feel like hitting up downtown Chicago at that point, so I headed to the closest coffee shop. I sat there drinking coffee and feeling awful. I tried to direct my focus elsewhere, but I could think of nothing else. I knew I couldn't pay for my costly mistake, but I wish I had at least offered up that information.

I decided to send Candy a message. She had been at work all day and had no idea what had happened. I explained the toilet situation and let her know how terribly sorry I was. I explained my finances, saying that I wanted to pay but simply could not. Her response was immediate and heartfelt. It was also filled with the laughter of a computer keyboard. She told me not to worry about the toilet. She pointed out that it was an accident, something that could have happened to anyone. It was her plea that I not agonize over the cost, saying that she would not want me to pay for the damage even if I were able. I was encouraged by her computer laughter and thankful for her understanding.

On my last night in Chicago, my host family (proud owners of a brand-new toilet) invited me out for dinner. We ate, talked, and laughed. My toilet trouble was a silly joke rather than the point of contention I was once worried it would be. At the end of our meal, my friends asked if they could pay for my meal. The price of the meal was certainly within my budget, but they would not take no for an answer.

We all headed to our cars, and said our goodbyes. As I began to prepare for my drive to the next location on my map, Candy handed me an envelope and bid me well. I headed out on the road, but decided to pull over and open the envelope. Inside was a card, thanking me for spending the week with them. They were grateful to be a part of my journey for a week. That's right, the family that opened their home and allowed me to intrude on their lives for an entire week had given me a thank-you card. If that weren't enough, inside the heart-warming card was a prepaid gift card for $150, basically the same amount it cost to replace the toilet I had destroyed. I had no words. I was completely caught off guard.

I had cost them so much: not only the toilet repairs, but the day of missed work it took to complete the repairs. I made a mess and they gave me a gift?

Love like that is rare. That selfless, unconditional, and unharnessed kind of love is found in so few. That love should never, ever be taken for granted.

I called Candy right away. I thanked her for her kindness and generosity, and expressed my shock and confusion. I also let her know that if she wanted to pay me to break anything else, I'd be more than willing.

-DANCE DANCE ABIGAIL-OUTION-

In Toronto I had the privilege of meeting the daughter of two dear friends of mine. She was a very sweet girl and her name was Abigail. Let me tell you something about Abigail.

She loved to dance.

She was pretty stinking cute, too. I will give her that. Maybe it was that blond hair? Or those blue eyes? I honestly don't know, but she most certainly loved to dance. Her voice was very nasally when she spoke. It wasn't a voice that was hard on the ears, but rather one that drew you in. Listening to her speak was almost addictive. I found myself looking for ways to keep her talking. And her laugh? It was as if God had created that laugh just for her.

She was so real. She was naive, honest, and just full of life. She was so full of life that she could barely contain it. It often seemed like she had to work really hard just to keep up with herself, and she was only seven years old.

She was constantly on the go. Her activities of choice were all lively: moving, talking, laughing, and dancing. Boy, did we dance. Over, and over, and over again, we twirled, spun, kicked, and flailed. She had me play song after song on my computer so that she could continue to show me more of her moves. These moves had clearly been stored down deep in her soul, waiting for just the right moment to surface.

It was extremely difficult to tell her no. Even when I found myself wanting to move on to another task, she would push for "just one more" song. It was impossible to refuse. If I tried, she gave me "the Look." "The Look" was pulled from a very special place and was put on display only in the most desperate of situations. It was reserved for those times when she wanted to get her way. When she wanted to dance. And it worked. I was unable to say no, and then...she had me right where she wanted me: on her own little dance floor.

I began to tire, but we continued to dance.

I began to feel silly, but we continued to dance.

I began to not want to dance, but...we continued to dance.

She laughed, and laughed, and laughed, and laughed. And we danced, and danced, and danced, and danced.

I could not help but smile. I could not help but laugh. I could not help but...dance.

In spite of the difficulties I was dealing with in my life, I found myself momentarily forgetting about my "issues" and simply appreciating the moment that I had with this little dance guru. It brought me pure joy to dance with this sweet little ball of energy. Her happiness reminded me of what real, innocent happiness is all about. Her laughter resurrected an authentic joy that I had allowed to die.

I watched her passionately put everything that she had into each and every one of her moves. I observed as she lived her life to the fullest, untainted by the scars that come with age. I was inspired by her desire to simply just live and to dance. She gave me fuel and branded me with her joy. And she had no comprehension of the impression that she left on me.

It has been months since the last time that I saw her. Since those moments, I have acquired new scars. I've been reminded of the destructiveness of people and the distinctiveness of the past. I have stared straight into the face of disease and dealt with the discomfort of illness. These things have sought to rob me of my joy and consume my existence.

Daily life has continued to prove unfair. But, I continue to carry the memory of those simple moments spent dancing, and the deeper meaning that I drew from them. When I look back, I cannot help but smile. I cannot help but laugh. I cannot help but...dance.

-NO HEART FEELINGS-

My time spent in downtown Toronto was one of the coolest parts of my journey. Maybe part of it was the fact that I had successfully taken my journey all the way to another country.

When I met my friends Melissa and Tanji, I was somewhere around downtown. I had specifically headed to that area because I wanted to meet a younger crowd. I had walked into a coffee shop by random selection. It was not very big, but its audience suggested it was "big." I assumed it was one of the cooler shops in the area due to the steady flow of traffic coming in and out. I ordered my usual Americano and headed to a seat. As I sat down to drink my coffee, I pulled out my laptop to attempt to write. After many failed attempts to connect to what I thought was this establishment's WiFi, I was forced to stop a passing barista and ask for help. He informed me that they actually didn't have WiFi, by choice. Their goal was to create an environment less focused on individuality and more focused on community. As a person who seeks community, I thought the philosophy was fairly brilliant. So I tucked my laptop away and turned to face the room.

Sipping my Americano, I took a look around and noticed that the lack of WiFi didn't stop people from finding ways to distract themselves. There were people on their phones, people reading books, and people studying. There wasn't a person in the coffee shop without some sort of task at hand. Not wanting to interrupt any of the other patrons, I finished my drink and headed out of the shop. I didn't quite feel like a failure, but I felt a bit dissociated having not made any connections. On my way out the door, the name of the coffee shop printed on the outside of the window caught my eye. I stopped for a moment to take it in and noticed something else: In front of the window sat a stone bench. On the stone bench sat a really pretty girl.

I made a beeline for the bench and took a seat. There was enough space between us that my sudden arrival wasn't awkward. It was a bench and I was only occupying a portion of its space. No big deal, right? Anyhow, I pulled out my phone and acted like I was using it. I couldn't *actually* use my phone because one, my phone wouldn't work in Canada and two, there was no WiFi. I decided to take a picture of the coffee shop's decal in the window so I could remember having been there. I also used this as an opportunity to open up a conversation.

"Uh, excuse me, just so you know, I am only taking a picture of the window behind you. I am not some creepy dude trying to take a picture of the back of your head." For whatever reason, she thought that was funny and engaged in conversation. As we continued to talk, my attention was caught by an eccentric-looking man. He was extremely unique, but in a way that was very appealing. He had long, curly hair and was wearing children's colorful, heart-shaped sunglasses. He was mysterious and captivating. I couldn't help but acknowledge him. This desire was easily fulfilled when I found out he happened to be friends with the pretty girl I was currently speaking with.

Soon, the three of us were sitting on that magical bench and talking. I learned that the pretty girl's name was Melissa and she was from Canada. The eccentric man's name was Tanji, and he was from France. I will be honest and say that I do not remember the details of our conversation. I do remember that I was very much enjoying myself. As we continued to speak, Melissa stood and pulled a bottle of bubbles out of her bag. She proceeded to open the bubbles and blow them. I didn't really think much of it at the time, but it seems funny now. She paced back and forth for some time while blowing her bubbles, but soon started blowing them toward the people passing by. She didn't blow them in their faces, she playfully lined their path. Perhaps it was the fact that she was super cute, or perhaps everyone she encountered just liked bubbles, but she got away with her bubble antics. Melissa got a lot of looks, most of which were smiles. Many people didn't say anything, but some said, "Hello." I began to wonder if her act of silliness had any sort of a deeper effect on the people walking by. I wondered if she was improving anyone's day.

I couldn't help admiring Melissa. Sure, she was just blowing bubbles, but something about her actions took bravery. She didn't care what people thought, she just wanted to make them smile. She took her hijinks to a different level when she reached back into her magic bag and pulled out a sheet of stickers. I looked closely and realized they were tiny heart stickers. She began handing them out to people as they walked down the street.

Melissa would stop them for a moment and ask if she could give them a sticker. Most people smiled and said, "Sure." She got a few rejections, but she didn't let that get her down. Men and women of all ages received stickers that day. Very few declined.

There was one man whose name I never learned but face I'll never forget. For the sake of the story, we'll call this man Bueller. Bueller was probably around sixty years old. He walked with a limp. He was wearing khaki pants and a dress shirt. He was one of those cute older men that you would expect to see at the same diner every day. He had big metal glasses, bushy eyebrows, and a squishy face. His bottom lip sort of sunk into his mouth, while his top lip exposed his teeth.

He was making his way down the street when he was approached by my new friend with the stickers. He seemed confused when this lovely young woman said hello to him. Her genuine smile and sincere eyes would be slightly startling. Even if Bueller wasn't a people person, there was no way he would be able to escape the web of her kindness. He stopped when she spoke and pulled his eyes up from their gaze at the ground. Melissa smiled and asked if he would like a sticker. He looked confused, but also a bit flattered. He asked her, "Why?" Without missing a beat, she explained that he was a beautiful person and her stickers were beautiful heart stickers sent to remind him of such. She seemed to spew positivity. He looked at her, then looked over to Tanji and me, still a bit confused. I spoke up and reassured Bueller that the words she spoke were true, but there was no pressure to take the sticker. Tanji said, "It's true, you don't have to if you do not want to. There will be no heart feelings." ("No *heart* feelings"—you see what he did there?)

Bueller then looked up at Melissa, pulled a tan-colored hat out of his bag, and said, "Okay, but will you put it on my hat?" Melissa continued to maintain that one-of-a-kind beautiful smile of hers as she took Bueller up on his offer and delicately placed a heart sticker on his hat. In response to this Bueller looked down at his hat and back toward us. He then looked at his hat and back toward us again. And then, he said words that I will never forget: "Thanks guys, I really need to think better of myself." After that, he thanked each one of us, and continued on his way down the road.

As he walked away, there was a look in his eyes that I will never forget. It was clear that our words and actions had affected him. Before his meeting with us, Bueller appeared to be making his way down the street with what looked to be the face of a man who was sad, lonely, and in pain. But, as he walked away, he appeared to have a small glimpse of hope in his eyes.

It's very clear to me this encounter had put that little sparkle in his eyes. This moment and the resulting sparkle are things that I will never forget. This experience reminded me that nothing in life mattered more than just simply loving people.

-BORDER PO-PO-TROL-

Getting into Canada was easy. I pulled up to the border crossing guard and handed him my passport. He looked at me, looked at my passport, and then looked at me. He asked me one question: "Do you have any guns?" I did not, so I was sent on my way. I found it slightly funny that they would ask such a serious question and not take any sort of visual account of the contents of my vehicle. What if I did have guns?

Those thoughts quickly drifted from my mind when I realized that I was in Canada! I had been to Canada once, but I had simply crossed over from Detroit onto the southern tip of the country. I didn't think that really counted as going to Canada. This time, I was headed for Toronto. I had actually never even driven in "another country" before, so I was pretty stoked about the entire experience.

I was in and I was on my way.

One week later, I learned the difference between crossing the border from the United States to Canada vs. crossing the border from Canada to the United States. It was a Sunday; a nasty, rainy Sunday. I was really tired. My GPS wasn't working, so I was forced to use old-fashioned paper directions. My friend had helped me map out the best directions, but I still managed to get lost. I decided to pull over at a rest stop to stretch, grab a drink, and connect to WiFi. I used my phone to find a new route out of Canada so I could make my way to my next stop. I soon started seeing signs for the border, as well as signs for Niagara Falls. Part of me really wanted to stop and check out the Falls, while the other part wanted to keep going and try to make up for the time I had already lost. Part of me was also conflicted because I had heard that if you are going to experience the Falls, you *have* to do it from the Canadian side. I was informed that it was *so* much better, since...you actually get to see the water falling. I figured I had time to make up my mind considering that the Falls were still a good distance off.

As I continued to drive through Canada, I kept passing signs pointing in the direction of the Falls. Despite the fact that I was going to be late in my arrival to my next destination, I simply could not resist. I might not ever have this chance again, was my thought. I decided to stop on the Canadian side and experience one of those "you have to do this if you ever get a chance" opportunities.

I am so glad that I stopped. I didn't stay long, but I was there long enough to have my breath taken away. It was stunning. Mesmerizing to say the least. I walked around, took some pictures, and soaked in the sights. I also got soaked to the bone because it was raining.

I headed back to my car and made my way out of the Falls area. I somehow got turned around, and wasn't sure if I was headed in the right direction. I saw an employee area and stopped to ask which way I should head. I hated having to ask for help. I am a man! I don't ask for help! Plus, I was exhausted, sweaty, and soaking wet; all I wanted to do was get to my next city! I mumbled my request, and the kind young lady directed me where to go.

I finally pulled up to border patrol and handed them my passport. In return, they handed me a piece of paper and requested that I enter a nearby building. I asked if everything was alright, and they told me that I needed to talk to the people inside. I grew concerned. Leaving my passport behind with the not-so-friendly patrolman, I headed inside.

At this point in my story, I have a bit of a confession to make. The night before this incident, I was out very late with a Canadian friend that I met in Korea and a group of her friends. I was out so late that, when I arrived at the subway and showed them my day pass, it was denied.

I was more than certain that the time had not run out on my pass, and tried to explain that I should still be able to use it. They disagreed, did not allow me to use it, and insisted that I pay for another pass.

I felt like maybe they were trying to pull one over on me. (Silly, I know, but I was convinced that I could use my pass up until like five in the morning before I needed to use a different one, and it was only like two.)

I was left in somewhat of an awkward position. I had already met my transportation budget for the week, and my trip budget was already super tight. I found it difficult to justify the purchase of another pass since I would be leaving the next day. Oh, and...I couldn't call on my host for the week because he had left town, so I was flying solo at his shack.

I started walking, heading away from my stop. I wandered around the area, wondering what I would do next. I saw people coming out of the exit, and then...a light bulb turned on inside my head. It was a crazy idea, but I decided to go with it.

The people exiting the subway had to go through exit gates with metal counters. While standing in that area, I could see the man who had denied my day pass. He was facing the direction of all those entering into this part of the subway. He had his back to me. I waited and watched. Was I really going to do this? My chest was pounding. What if I got caught?

I took a deep breath and took off running. I placed my hands on the top of the exit gate and vaulted to the other side. I continued running until I found the train that I needed to board to make my way back home. I felt slightly guilty, but my day pass was paid for and usable. I should have been allowed access, so...I accessed!

Now, back to the border. With a twinge of guilt hanging in the back of my mind, I continued my walk toward the building. Had they found out about my adventures in the subway system? Was I in trouble? I know presuming that they knew anything about the previous night was a long stretch, but that's where my head was at the moment.

I entered a large room. Each footstep echoed loudly as I made my way across the open, empty space. It seemed like I walked a mile before I made my way up to a desk where three people sat. These people, two men and one woman, were dressed in full uniform. One of the men asked me why I was in Canada. I told him that I had always wanted to visit Canada and a friend had invited me to visit. He said, "Okay, but why Canada?" I told him a bit about my journey, visiting cities and sharing the story of my plight with cancer with those I met. He again replied, "Why Canada?"

I responded again, telling him that I had the opportunity to add his country as a destination on my journey, and I didn't want to pass it up. He again said, "Why Canada?" —This is *not* a joke. I seriously began to wonder if this was a trick question. He finally changed his tune, but asked me to empty my pockets.

I took out my phone, wallet, and keys, and I placed them on the counter. He picked them all up and locked them in a box. The Canadian border authorities now had my keys, wallet, phone, passport, and my car full of possessions.

He then asked me to sit down. *At least he didn't say, "Why Canada?" again,* I thought to myself as I took a seat. I sat for less than ten minutes before I noticed armored members of the border patrol and their canine counterparts checking my car outside. *Do these people think I have drugs?* I stifled a bit of a laugh because, well, I am Cooper! If they knew me, they wouldn't have even made me get out of my car! I am the last guy who would be attempting to smuggle drugs. I then remembered the state of my appearance and understood that it could be misleading. A late night, a skipped shower, a long car ride, a walk in the rain. Heck, I couldn't even remember if I had brushed my teeth that morning. Oh, Canada. Haven't you ever had one of those days?

I was eventually released and allowed to head back to the homeland.

So... If you're ever headed to Canada, remember this: Getting in, suuuuuuper easy (unless you answer "yes" to the gun question, I assume). But, here's a bit of advice for the trip home: be sure to shower. Brush your hair. Put on some fresh clothes and clean kicks. Oh, and brush your teeth, so you can use your million-dollar smile as leverage for entry back into your own country.

-FRIED CHICKEN, GUMBO, AND UNCLE STEVE-

I handed him the small box. To some, it would be an offensive gesture, but to him? It was like he had won the lottery.

When I met him, I had just left a restaurant where I was having dinner with a good friend and host for the week, Lindsay. It was her desire that I experience Eugene, Oregon, in the most raw and organic way possible. She only recommended hole-in-the-wall type places: those shops and restaurants so rich with culture, they provided experience in addition to sustenance. This restaurant ranked high on her list. According to her, it served "soul food."

When we arrived, I was greeted by a hanging sign reading "Papa's Soul Food Kitchen and BBQ." Their tagline was, "Tastes so good it'll make you want to slap yo' mama!!" I wasn't sure about *that*, but I was certainly ready for some finger-licking good food. We were soon inside at a small table, checking out the menu. Available were a collection of home-cooked southern meals, including soul food, BBQ, and Louisiana-style Cajun or Creole. I was excited to try some fried chicken with a side of three-buck mac and cheese. You know I am a major coffee snob, but you may not know that I'm also a fried chicken snob. It has to be crispy and juicy with just the right punch of flavor. I was feeling optimistic about this choice.

Lindsay, who tends to be shy yet adventurous, was eyeing the gumbo. She had never tried Cajun food of any kind before, so I offered up some of my experiences as encouragement. The family I lived with while I underwent cancer treatment had introduced me to New Orleans cuisine. The mother was actually from Louisiana and created amazing gumbo. I had become a big fan of all flavors Cajun, and relayed this information to Lindsay.

Our food arrived, and I am pleased to relay that Papa's fried chicken plus mac and cheese blew my expectations out of the water. Sadly, my dear friend was not as pleased with her selection. Gumbo, it seems, was just not her thing. I felt bad, having assumed that she would love it as much as I did. I also felt bad enjoying my food so thoroughly when she was obviously not. Regardless of what was happening on our plates, we enjoyed our time talking.

Feeling as though I had eaten an entire chicken and five pounds of macaroni, I looked down at my plate. It appeared as though I had barely touched the generous portion of food. I was completely ready to keep eating away, but I felt bad that Lindsay's food experience had ended soon after it began. Not wanting to make her sit and watch me devour the rest of my meal, I requested a to-go box. I would have delicious leftovers to look forward to the next day. She got a box as well, but planned on finding someone else to enjoy her meal instead.

As we headed out of the restaurant, boxes in hand, we explored the area for a few minutes. Side note: If you've never been to Eugene, I highly recommend it. It is, by far, one of my favorite cities in North America. The people are kind, the places are intriguing, and the scenery is beautiful. As we walked that night, we were approached by a man. I never got his real name, but somewhere along the way I decided to call him Uncle Steve. Steve was pulling a wagon with what appeared to be everything he owned on the inside, including his dog. I liked him right away. He was a soulful older man. He was kind in his approach to others. He wasn't looking to take advantage of those around him. I was met with the feeling that he was simply a man in the midst of a difficult season. I felt like I had a deeper understanding of his situation. Currently, I didn't have a home per se. I was in a constant state of travel. But Uncle Steve didn't have friends to host him. He was looking for assistance.

If you've paid any attention at all, you know that I'm poor. I wasn't able to hand out money as I wished. I did try to help out in other "creative" ways along my journey. As much as I wanted to share my meager financial rations with Uncle Steve, I knew that it would push my budget way off-track. I looked down at the box in my hand. My fried chicken and macaroni goodness sat snugly inside. I was so looking forward to those leftovers. Cold fried chicken holds a section of my heart hostage, and this chicken was some of the best.

Lindsay, with no hesitation, offered Steve her gumbo. She had packed up her to-go box with the intention of finding someone else to enjoy it. I, on the other hand, had packed mine up to be devoured by me later. His response to her offer was memorable. He could likely feel the warmth of the food inside as he took it in his hands. He expressed genuine gratitude, for he and his dog would eat well that night.

His kindness and grateful declarations were giant slaps in my chicken-loving face. Seeing the joy provided by a single serving of gumbo, I knew that I had to hand over my box. As I offered the last of my meal, Steve's face lit up. It was as if I had read the final number on a winning Powerball ticket. He was so thankful. He praised our generosity and kindness. As painful as it had been to hand over that food, it was such a small gesture. I would have food readily available to me the next day, even if it wasn't five-star fried chicken. Uncle Steve would be back out on the streets, dependent on the generosity of others, yet he was thankful beyond measure for those boxes of leftover food.

Uncle Steve was living in the shadow of a series of unfortunate events. Nonetheless, he was passionate about life. In his brokenness, he was simple and real. He was loving and kind. His willingness to care for others in spite of his current circumstance was shown by the care he gave to his dog.

For whatever reason, I've always wanted an Uncle Steve. Now that I finally have one, I will do my best to carry on the legacy he unknowingly created.

-THE INTERVIEW-

I magine yourself in a coffee shop. It's a hole-in-the-wall sort of place you have grown attached to. All of the staff members boast their own form of artistic flair. Each one greets you with a welcoming spirit. They naturally carry on conversations. Not chats about the weather, but deep talks about real life. On top of that, you happen to be drinking some of the best coffee in the country, alongside a bowl of the tastiest oatmeal you've ever eaten. You must be in Eugene, Oregon, at The Wandering Goat.

During my week in Eugene, The Wandering Goat felt like home. Each day, I spent a few hours there, later heading to the brewery across the street. Both establishments provided pleasant experiences and people to connect with. It was easy to begin conversations with people in Eugene. Perhaps there was something in the air. Maybe it had something to do with all that organic eating? Who knows.

It was a day like every other spent there. I had finished my time at The Wandering Goat and headed across the street to see whom I could meet. As I sat examining the room, I noticed a lady heading up to the counter. I listened as she and the man behind the counter discussed local beers. The one she ended up ordering came in a bottle the size of Florida. As she headed back to her table, I smiled and said, "Can you really handle all of that?" She wrestled the mammoth of a bottle to one side and assured me that her friends would be more than willing to help if she were unable. I must have stuck out as non-Eugenian, because she hung around for a few minutes and asked what I was doing in the area. A few sentences later, she was inviting me over to her table.

As I sat chatting with my new friends, I couldn't help but chuckle on the inside. If I had learned anything thus far on my journey, I knew I had the ability to connect with a large variety of people. These people happened to be quite a bit older than me, but that put no damper on our conversation. We talked about traveling and music. I found out that the two men were DJs for a local NPR radio station. As we continued to talk, we landed on the topic of cancer. I shared my story, and found out I wasn't the only one at the table with experience. One of the DJs, Eric, had his own bout with the disease. We swapped words of diagnoses, prognoses, and treatment. As horrible as cancer is, it tends to bring people together. We had a deeper understanding of each other in a short period of time because of that one commonality. He understood my journey, and my search for the deepest importance. I felt that I could learn a lot from this veteran of not only cancer, but life itself.

My three new friends seemed enticed by my desire to travel, meet people, and share my experience. I was caught off guard when Eric asked what I was doing the next day. I told him of my unscheduled ways, lacking plans and procedures. He then asked if he could interview me on the radio. Uhhh, what? Me? I looked over at that Florida-sized bottle of beer to see just how much he had been drinking. It was still fairly intact. My new friend informed me that he was inspired by my story, and thought it needed to be heard by more people. I couldn't believe it, but agreed to meet him at the station the next day.

I excused myself from the table and left the brewery feeling like I was floating in the clouds. I was so excited. I barely slept when I returned to my home of the week. I couldn't wait to sit behind a microphone and share my story. I also couldn't wait to tell my friends!

I pulled into the radio station the next day in my little car with Illinois license plates, rocking my skinny jeans and flannel shirt. I held my chest high as I walked into the station, feeling like I was a star. Ninety seconds later...I felt like a little boy who had wet his pants. I was *so* nervous. I felt anxious. I began to feel full of doubt. I was terrified that my story would have no effect on anyone. I was concerned that I'd sound like a fool behind the mike. I also hoped I was not a charity case, wasting the time and energy of my new friend.

Moments later, I was finally in place and behind the microphone when Eric started asking me questions. He asked what I had learned from my experience with cancer. He asked me about my journey, Coffee with Cooper, and how it began. The questions continued, and I answered each one to the best of my ability. I remember talking, but I also remember thinking everything coming out of my mouth was gibberish.

Let's face it: I have the gift of gab. Talking to people is not difficult for me, and sharing my story provided ample opportunities for just that. These questions had been asked multiple times in the past months, and the answers usually flowed naturally. But as I found myself behind this microphone, it appeared as though I had lost the ability to formulate complete sentences that made any sense. I was doubting myself and the strength of my words. At the most inconvenient time, I found myself wondering if what I was saying would even be interesting to listeners. Did I sound like an idiot? Was Eric regretting his decision to bring me here?

I knew that wasn't the case, but convincing myself was hard. I gave myself a moment to take a breath. I had been diagnosed with terminal cancer. I wasn't dead or even quickly dying. I was alive and on the move. I had a *story* to tell.

Eric finished asking his questions, and I did my best to answer effectively. As we wrapped up, he told me the interview would be edited and pieced together in a way that flowed well for listeners. Perhaps he could feel my insecurities, or perhaps that's just how it goes. My doubt told me that the former was true.

The next day, I heard myself on the radio. Eric had done what he said he would. He used his magic touch to make me sound almost human. His editing gave my words a certain flow they seemed to lack during my time behind the microphone. It really wasn't too bad!

To my surprise, I started receiving notes from people who had heard my interview. They popped onto the Coffee with Cooper page and let me know that they had enjoyed hearing my story. Some listeners even "liked" my page so they could follow along with the rest of my journey.

My story is a good one. My story can inspire and lead to change in other people. Why do I have to remind myself of this so often? Why does any person doubt their ability to do anything (within reason), really?

My interview may not have gone viral and gained millions of followers for my page, but it reminded me that my doubt is out of place. My story is a good one. And I was meant to share it.

Another belief was also reinforced from this experience: we need to surround ourselves with good people. We need friends around us who are willing to step up and help in the areas where we are lacking. Eric heard my story and knew it would be more valuable the farther it spread. My reach was three people around the table in a brewery in Eugene. He expanded that reach to all of Oregon's KLCC listeners. He also kept me from sounding like a mumbling idiot. Each doing what we loved, together we created something inspiring. My passion combined with his radio reach (and the magic of editing) touched more lives than I ever imagined there in Oregon.

* If you'd like to hear that interview, just google coffeewithcooper KLCC Eugene, Oregon.
The page I refer to in the interview is no longer one that I use, but the interview is still very much accessible.

-THE PLUNGE I NEVER TOOK-

Sometimes my eyes are bigger than my stomach. Too often I say words before I think about them. I think we've all had our fair share of these moments. I would like to say I learned a valuable lesson from each of my own moments, but that would probably be a lie. I can, without a doubt, say I learned from an experience during my time in Boulder, Colorado.

Boulder is an amazingly beautiful place. The scenery looks other-worldly, and the city is full of rich culture, great food, and wonderful people. I had no problem making friends in Boulder. Conversation happened often and flowed effortlessly. I felt like my story moved through the people there with ease, and hope spread like moss. My week in Boulder was, by far, one of my favorites.

During my time there, I stayed with a guy I knew from college. We weren't close during our time at school, but we were well acquainted. As soon as I arrived, I felt warmly welcomed by him and his girlfriend. They showed interest in who I was and all I had been through, and also sought to help me experience Boulder to the fullest. They had already made plans for my first night in town, which was to be spent hiking. Colorado is obviously one of the best places for hiking and many people were drawn there for that very reason. I had done some hiking while I lived in Korea, but I had never been a part of a real, American hiking experience.

I knew the scenery would be striking, but I soon learned that, at its climax, this hike held an extra surprise. When you reached the top of the mountain (which, by the way, was one of the most majestic scenes I've ever taken in) you were greeted by an icy lake. Snow collected in the mountains year after year, and this lake was formed. The water was colder than you could ever imagine. Many people made the hike with one goal: jump in that water. They would plunge through the frigid surface just to see how long they could withstand the brutal temperature.

I tend to be a bit of a thrill-seeker and was feeling up for the challenge. Together we would hike. Together we would take the plunge.

As we headed up the mountain, I was overwhelmed by the towering trees, the sounds of animals, and the feeling of earth under my feet. The hike was a heavenly experience. I soaked up every moment, wanting to experience every sight and smell to the fullest. We were excited to reach the top, but there was no need to rush.

Along the way up the mountain, we discussed the adventure that lay ahead. My host for the week did his best to hype us up, asking every once in a while if we were ready to take the plunge. We. Were. Ready.

We soon reached the top. It was stunning. I could see for miles. The sky was blue and bright. The trees were the greenest green, and taller than any I had seen. And directly in front of me, nestled twenty feet below, was the most terrifying body of water I ever set eyes on. It was crystal clear, revealing the rocky floor below. I could feel the cold radiating from the surface. My friend looked around and asked if we were ready. My body felt like it weighed one million pounds. I couldn't move my feet or even speak. All I could think was, *If I jump in there, I am going to die.* Before I could respond, he had jumped.

I stood and watched his body soar through the air. It was like one of those slow motion movie scenes where you are frozen in time, watching someone else inch closer to doom. All we could do was stare.

His body finally made contact, and was quickly submerged in the icy water. I remember the look of shock on his face as he came back to the surface. I thought he might cry, but he suddenly let out a shout of victory. He had done it.

He made his way out of the water and back up to where his girlfriend and I stood. I tried to convince myself that I could do this, but seemed to be failing. I did not want to jump. Well, I did...but I didn't. I secretly hoped his girlfriend would chicken out so it would be easier for me to say no. I am all about gender equality in everyday life, but I could not let myself be shown up by a girl in this situation. My friend could tell that we were feeling overwhelmed and tried to encourage us. He reminded us that we had hiked up a mountain just for this. He told us that it was horribly cold, but totally worth it. The next thing I knew, she jumped.

There I stood, at the top of a mountain. I was dry. I was warm. I wanted to take the plunge, but my desire to stay put was stronger. Despite my two wet, cold friends encouraging me to step up to the challenge, the fear within me took over. I just couldn't do it. I was mad at myself. Had I really come all of this way to back down? I would probably never have this chance again. Was I going to let it pass me by? Yes. Yes, I was.

I collected my things and prepared for the journey back down the mountain. I felt like a failure. When introduced with the challenge, my talk had been big. I felt confident and ready to conquer anything and everything. I looked that test straight in the face and...let fear get the best of me. Despite the evidence that I would not die, I didn't jump. Regardless of the encouragement from those around me, I gave in to my doubt.

As I made the descent to the car, I began to reflect on my choice. I realized that giving up in the face of adversity had happened more than once. Actually, it was a fairly common reaction for me. In my normal, everyday life, I am surrounded by a strong community of friends. They support and encourage me when they see the need. They regularly challenge me to grow as a person, but I often chicken out. I have missed out on so many opportunities to stretch and mold a better me through experience by allowing fear to take over. I watch others set and meet goals, but don't believe I can do the same.

Possible consequences have prevented me from taking risks. Some of those risks could have been rewarding. Many risks could be positively life-changing, but my trepidation got in the way. Those moments are fleeting, and their departure is enduring.

I learned a lot from that experience. Yes, I wish I had taken the plunge that day, but I had to move on from the moment on the mountain. I will always carry the consequences of my choice, but I won't allow them to define me. Going forward, I hope to home in on moments like those. I want to stand up to my fear, grab ahold of those once-in-a-lifetime opportunities, and allow myself to be changed by them. There are many plunges I never took, but the ones that have yet to arrive are my focus.

-THE COUSIN THAT CHANGED-

When Coffee with Cooper began, I had one tattoo. At journey's end, I had four. Having read this book, you're likely to wonder how on earth I managed to pay for three more tattoos. I will admit, that is a very fair inquiry (especially if you donated money to support my endeavors). In all honesty, I didn't pay a cent for them. They were free. Only the best things in life come at zero cost, right? Okay, when it comes to tattoos, that is obviously not usually the case. But my "case" has special circumstances.

After leaving Albuquerque (and before arriving in Manhattan, Kansas) I made a little pit stop to see a cousin of mine. His name is Brad, and he is a great guy. Brad grew up in an environment that likely influenced many of the choices that he'd make later in life. He followed in the footsteps of those around him, and they led him to jail. When he was released, freedom never lasted long. Brad made countless promises to stop making the same foolish choices, but his promises were fleeting.

There was only one thing that he was better at than getting into trouble: sketching. He was a fantastic artist. I remember visiting my grandmother during holidays and hearing her rave about his ability to create beautiful, realistic art. I don't know where he inherited that talent, but...he was gifted. Through years of addiction and life lived in and out of prison, the only healthy outlet Brad had was art.

As he aged, Brad tried to be a good father to his two children, but his choices made that nearly impossible. He was often more concerned with getting his next fix than being a husband and father for his family. This is, after all, what he had experienced as a child in his own home. I am sure there were loving "family moments" in his own childhood and the lives of his young children, but I fear that they were few and far between.

During one long prison stay, something happened to Brad. I don't know if it was the thought of spending the rest of his life in prison or the realization that he would lose his wife and children, but something deep within him began to move. His wife had informed him that she was relocating from Missouri to Arizona with their two children. She had also informed him that she was willing to wait for his release. I believe her love and willingness to stand by her husband in the worst of times changed him in a big way. He realized that his choices had consequences for his family. Brad's focus became being a better man.

He spent the rest of his time in prison releasing himself from addiction's grasp. He started focusing on his art and looked for ways to improve it. When his sentence was served, he headed to Arizona where his family was waiting, as promised. They welcomed him with open arms.

I can't imagine what it felt like to be released from prison and gain acceptance from the family you abandoned by choice. I deeply respect Brad's wife for sticking by his side. She must have seen beyond his bad choices to the man that he could be, with the hope that he would someday see it, too.

This time, Brad kept his promise. He got a job in construction. He worked hard to provide for his family, but full-time work wasn't currently available to him or his co-workers. He knew that he had to find a way to compensate for the lack of hours his job was able to provide. He also knew that he needed to stay busy in a healthy and constructive way. He fell back on the only other positive outlet in his life: art. Was there a way that he could profit from his love for drawing?

Brad began looking for possible side work as an artist. He found a local tattoo shop with an available apprenticeship. It would be a gamble, since there was no hourly pay. He would only be paid if he created art on the body of another. To make his ability known, Brad began offering small tattoos with a small price tag. The small tattoos would become his billboards. People would see his work in small scale and (hopefully) his clientele would increase.

My cousin had honed his artistic ability. He knew that this type of artistry would require a lot of learning, but he was prepared to do whatever it took. And that's exactly what he did. Tattooing became his new addiction. It drove his energy and passion in a new, healthy direction. He could do what he loved and hopefully support his family in the process.

Brad became such a talented and well-known artist that he was able to open his own tattoo shop. He went from an imprisoned addict to a successful business owner. He saved his marriage, developed relationships with his children, and repaired the ties with his extended family. Art literally saved his life. That and real love.

I am thankful to be a billboard for my cousin's work. His work tells the story that I want it to, but it also reflects his story. Both stories carry power and deserve to be made known.

My goal as I traveled was to use my story to inspire others. That inspiration was often reciprocated through the stories of others. Cancer, addiction, loss...from all of these tragedies came something beautiful. They create a language by which we are able to communicate with the world around us. What holds us back from sharing those moments with others?

-DINNER WITH AN ANGEL-

She stood in her kitchen making dinner for the group of familiar faces that would shortly arrive. There were tears in her eyes and streaks of mascara on her face. Despite the weight that consumed her heart, she stood her ground. She was so strong. She was so sweet. She was an angel.

I remember the first time I met her. She extended her hand to formally introduce herself. I noticed right away that there was an honesty in her eyes, and that it was mixed with something else. It was something familiar. It was the look of someone facing something extremely painful. I could feel so deeply that she was desperately fighting to hold on. I knew in that moment that she didn't need a handshake; I knew that she needed a hug. So, I hugged her. She was a good hugger. No, she was a *great* hugger. Her hug was real. It was not halfhearted. She put everything she had into that hug. After getting to know her, I am now convinced that she puts everything she has into everything she does.

The group arrived as planned and I found myself surrounded by people I am happy to call my friends. We sat there eating as our host shared with us about the most recent happenings in her life. She happily spoke of her job, and how much she enjoyed the day-to-day tasks that it presented. Her joy seemed cut short as she went on to share that her more than thirty years of marriage was coming to an end. Her husband had chosen to be unfaithful, and as a result they would no longer be married.

I could feel the depths of her emotions as she shared her pain and disappointment. I also couldn't help but notice that she did this with such an incredible grace and admirable strength.

And…as the old saying goes, "When it rains it pours."

This old phrase became an unfair reality for my sweet friend. Less than twenty-four hours after our meal together, she was fired from her job. This was the same job that, just hours before, she had been raving about. It was the same job that, much like her marriage, she had committed herself to fully. It was also the job I am certain she had hoped would become a distraction from her crumbling relationship. Not to mention it was the job that paid her bills.

I cannot help wondering why some people are dealt such horrible hands in life. Sometimes it seems like the best people, the most deserving ones, are dealt the worst hands. Why? Why did this hard-working, kind woman have to deal with such difficult situations? Why did she have to carry such a heavy weight on her shoulders?

I felt angry on her behalf. I had not known her very long, but I already looked at her much like I would my own mother—with respect! I did not approve of the way she was being treated. Why was she left struggling, with no room to breathe?

Honestly, the entire situation frustrated me and I wanted to take action. I wanted to find the man who had caused her so much pain and punch him straight in the face. I wanted to find the employer who told her she was not "performing at her best" (at quite possibly one of the *worst* times in her life) and punch him straight in the face.

Back when I first started telling people about my cancer, I remember having to tell them that it came with a 95% mortality rate. This was never an easy task. My words of doom were usually reciprocated by "the look." If you didn't read the intro (dude, you didn't read the intro yet!?), I will fill you in on "the look." First, the receivers of words get a glazed look in their eyes. This is usually followed by a lump in their throat, which they struggle to swallow. When that lump fails to dissipate, they sigh. No matter how hard they try to hold it in, it is almost always a long, airy, painful sigh, followed by…"the apology": "I am so sorry. I am so sorry. I wish I could think of something else to say, but…I don't know what else to say. I am just so sorry."

Looking back, I am genuinely thankful for each of the sincere moments that I had with my friends and family. I so very much appreciate their worry and sorrow that each of them carried on my behalf. But, in response to each of these sincere moments, I often found myself left standing with a sense of guilt. I did not want any of them to feel obligated to come up with a magical arrangement of words in an attempt to make me feel better. I never expected anyone to have the perfect thing to say in response to my diagnosis. I knew there were not any magical words that would fix my situation. There was nothing anyone could say that would change the fact that cancer had become part of my story.

Early on, I accepted the fact that this was now part of my life and at any point, anything could happen. I knew that I had the choice to allow this season to make or break me. I could use it, or I could let it use me. I knew that it wouldn't be easy and that I had a hell of a ride in front of me...but I also knew that the ride wasn't going to control the rider.

I continued to listen as my friend told me about her newest set of circumstances. Suddenly I found myself overwhelmed by a need to "say the right thing." I felt a pressure to relate to her. I felt a need to dig deep into my personal history purse and pull out a polished set of magical words, aka, "the solution to all of her problems."

In that moment, I was finally able to understand all the people I had spoken with about my sickness.

I finally knew what it felt like to feel a desire to cure another person's "disease" with fancy words.

But, I wasn't there to "fix" her problems. As nice as that would have been, the scenario wasn't close to being real. What was real, though, was the opportunity I had to play a small role of encouragement in her life. She didn't need me to butt in with some magical polished script. She needed me to be a friend and listen.

Her story is one that is far from over. Nothing about the blows she had to endure fell into category "easy." But, over time, I am convinced that she has learned to adjust.

Healing requires time, and the process, more times than not, can seem difficult, if not impossible, to endure. This part of her story might have been a sad one, but that does not mean it ended that way.

She is an incredible woman with an incredible story of strength. Many times since that meal I have received multiple notes of encouragement from her, motivating me during some difficult times in my life.

She lives to inspire. I am convinced that she will only continue to transition into something even more beautiful. I am positive that she will continue to do her best and allow nothing to hold her back from such.

She made the best of something awful. She set an example. She now has a unique opportunity to influence people who are going through similar situations. She now has a platform, and I have no doubt that she will use that to shine.

-THE GENTLE GIANT-

I want to do my best to tell this story. I want it to be authentic and genuine, just like it was in life. I want it to affect the reader in the same way it affected me. The story I now tell portrays an event that I think of daily. It was an event that touched me so deeply that I will likely think of it until the day that I die. How does one tell such a story? I guess there is no other place to start than at the beginning.

It was a day like any other. I was doing my thing, which probably involved drinking coffee. I remember scrolling through my Facebook feed, catching up on the everyday events in the lives of my friends. One thing that I really appreciate about social media is its ability to show you things from old friends that you haven't seen in a long time. You catch a picture with their familiar face or read a status that takes you down memory lane. On this particular day, I saw a post from a sweet girl named Rachel. Rachel was a girl I knew in college. Describing Rachel is simple: sweet, kind, meek, gentle, and genuine. Everyone needs a Rachel in their life.

Rachel's post that day caught my attention. She was requesting prayer for her older brother. His name was

Josh and he had just found out that he had cancer. I could feel the pain in Rachel's words as she asked her friends to pray for Josh. She wrote about her appreciation for her brother, and spoke of how much she loved and valued having him in her life. She loved her brother, and she could not imagine living in a world where he did not also live.

People across the world began praying for Josh. There was a page set up that allowed others to follow along with Josh on his fight against cancer. I joined with his family and friends in following his journey. I did not know Josh, but I understood his struggle in ways that most others could not.

I met a lot of people on my own journey who had personally dealt with cancer in one way or another. Each time, I was affected in a way that I really cannot describe. There is a strange connection between people who have or have had cancer. It is an instant bond. I experienced that bond several times along the road of Coffee with Cooper, but there was something about Josh's story that pulled at my heart. Knowing Rachel, and hearing of her love for her brother, made me want to be involved at a deeper level.

It all started with a simple note. I wrote to Rachel and I told her how sorry I was for the involvement that cancer now had in her life. I told her I was there for her, and that I would be praying. I also mentioned that I would be willing to talk to Josh if he were interested. I felt that I might be able to shed a tiny bit of light into the dark corners of life lived with cancer. I remembered the feelings and fears that arose when I received my own diagnosis. I wanted the opportunity to take all of the lessons that I learned and bring some encouragement to Josh.

Josh and I began our relationship with some pretty generic notes. We talked about our cancer and how we were diagnosed. We talked about the need for prayer while experiencing this new part of our lives. As I learned more about his life, I often found myself feeling bad. Things felt backwards to me. Josh was far worse off than I was. He was in the hospital while I was traveling across the United States. His diagnosis came out of nowhere. He was married and likely looking to start a family. I was very much single. I felt like the two of us should switch places. Why was he dealt a more difficult hand than me?

Josh and I continued writing. At times, it was difficult for him because he was often in a lot of pain, but he wrote when he could. My favorite thing about Josh was the fact that he didn't allow the pain he was experiencing to change who he was. The pain did nothing to deplete his joy. He didn't use it as an excuse. He never spoke out against God or lost his faith. He, experiencing so much pain and disappointment around every corner, used our messages to encourage me. At times, I was unhappy and struggling with my faith, and he would pick me up and dust me off. He reminded me what it meant to be a believer.

Josh "The Gentle Giant" would not be stopped. Josh was a big dude. He towered over most, standing six foot four and weighing 240 pounds. And then there was me: I am five foot eight and weigh 150. I wear skinny jeans and flannels. Josh: the man. Cooper: the boy. But Josh's Goliath-like stature carried an even larger heart: a heart that loved God, a heart that loved his family, a heart that loved his wife. Josh was so kind, caring, and loving toward all people. The nickname "The Gentle Giant" was every bit of fitting.

Josh was strong. Cancer tried to beat him down, but he refused to be a victim. On his darkest days, he was a light shining bright. I had pursued a relationship with Josh with the hopes of being an encouragement, yet here he was encouraging me and so many others around him. I had become comfortable in my position as a life-changer and I wasn't prepared for someone to so dramatically change mine.

In January of 2015, just months after Josh and I began speaking with each other, I received some devastating news. Josh was being sent home. His doctors had done all they could, but were unable to fight off the cancer. Reading the words hurt so bad. I cried for a long time. I was angry and I was sad. But Josh? He continued to be positive. He had moments of vulnerability and uncertainty, but he was always positive.

As Josh's condition worsened and he was sent home, I grew equally impressed with his wife, Annie. She was always positive and always honest. She spent a lot of time writing to friends and family on the Facebook page dedicated to Josh and his battle with cancer. The page was useful for sharing the latest updates, and for passing on well wishes and prayers. Annie also used the page to boast about her gentle giant. She spoke so fondly of him. She was proud of him and his strength, and spoke of his strength becoming her strength.

Despite being surrounded by the worst kind of chaos, Josh and Annie inspired and encouraged everyone around them. They willingly shared their daily struggles while it would have been so easy (and understandable) for them to hide away and grieve alone. They became this dynamic duo, quietly changing the world in a huge way.

When Josh was settled in his home, Annie sent out an invitation for people to come by and see him. She was unable to promise any visits because his condition changed from day to day. It was nearly impossible to predict how he would be feeling at any given time. However, she made it clear that they still wanted to visit with people whenever they were able.

It was strange for me to think about "meeting" Josh and Annie in person. I knew that I had only gotten to "know" Josh online, but I really felt like I knew him. We had personally written and received letters over the course of three months. I had kept up with every update and prayed faithfully for him and his family. I truly felt as though I had known him my entire life. When I heard that they were accepting visitors, I knew I needed to go. I was nearly 500 miles away, but I had to meet Josh in person. I had to thank him for investing his precious time and effort into me.

I wrote a message to Josh and Annie and asked if it would be appropriate for me to come for a visit. The response I received nearly broke me: "Cooper, I don't think that you will make it in time, but I really hope that you can make it to the memorial. I know that Josh would have wanted that."

I didn't understand why this was happening. Josh had been so faithful; why was cancer winning? Why was he being taken away like this? Why now?

Just a few days later, Josh passed away.

After that, I decided to make the trip. I needed to be there. Josh had done so much for me and I needed to pay my respects to him, to his wife, and to his sister, my dear friend. So I packed my bag and I headed to Cincinnati.

I was fortunate enough to arrive early and find a seat. There were quite a few people there to remember Josh and support his family. It was a beautiful service. It was obvious that he had heavily impacted so many lives. People shared thoughts about Josh. They grieved on his behalf. They laughed at memories they would forever carry with them. Josh was loved and would forever be remembered.

I don't believe that Annie's love for her husband was ever as evident as it was on that day. As she stood in front of the hundreds of people attending his service, you could see the love in her eyes. You could feel her pain: the pain of a woman who had been loved so deeply by a man who was now gone.

When Annie stood up to speak, she told a simple story. It was short, but powerful. Her story will forever stay with me. It was a day not long ago. Annie wasn't feeling well and her day just wasn't going right. Josh could tell that things were off, and he wanted to do what he had always done so naturally: he wanted to cheer her up. He decided that the two of them should go to the lake and feed the ducks. When he made the suggestion, Annie said that she just didn't feel like it. He refused to take no for an answer and persisted with his request. Despite his persistence, she had no desire to feed the ducks. Josh respected her wishes and decided to take a trip down to the lake himself. A short while later, Annie looked out the window to see her husband headed back toward their house. He was leading a pack of ducks along with him. If Annie didn't want to go down to the lake, Josh would bring the ducks to her!

It was Josh's desire that his wife always be full of joy. If she was having an "off" day, he would do everything in his power to turn it around. He loved her and he wasn't afraid to show it. He wanted her to know that she was loved, deep down, in a way that could last forever. As she stood and shared her story, it was evident that she did know. The pain she was feeling was real, but so was the love. Josh's love wasn't gone, and I believe it gave her the strength to continue standing.

Soon after Annie spoke, we were all invited to go outside and release balloons. It was a metaphorical way of letting Josh go. We may still mourn, but we could accept that he was now at home in Heaven. As we watched the balloons float upward, we sang a hymn in unison. It was a powerful moment that I will forever remember.

As of that moment, I had still not met Annie. I wanted to approach her and say something, but the right words were not there. I just kept thinking that everything I thought to say sounded cliché and halfhearted. Prior to the departure of the balloons, I looked up and saw her standing just twenty feet from me. I wanted to run up to her and hug her. I wanted to take away her pain. I wanted to express my love and appreciation for her and her husband. As her fist clenched her balloon, you could feel her trying to be strong. As she relaxed her fingers and let the balloon go, she silently mouthed, "Bye, Josh. I love you. I will see you soon."

After the departure of the balloons, we all went inside to have a meal together. I was able to find a few people that I knew, and decided to sit with them. As I sat at the table with Josh's sister Rachel and her husband, Rachel informed me that Annie really wanted to meet me. I was honored and terrified at the same time. What would I say?

As I stood in line waiting for my meal, I looked up and saw her talking to someone. She made eye contact with me and I knew there was no escape. But I wasn't ready! I hadn't yet formulated the words to say. So...I waved and walked toward her. Before saying anything, I simply hugged her. I had a flashback to the moments when I told people about my cancer diagnosis. *Insert deer in the headlights.* Did their shock and lack of words offend me? No. I knew that it was a difficult moment, and I realized I hadn't ever expected the perfect words. The fact that they cared was enough. I knew that this was the case now with Annie. My desire to "fix" her wasn't misplaced, but it wasn't realistic. She just needed support and comfort. So that is what I offered to the best of my ability.

As we talked, Annie told me that Josh had a strong desire to meet me. In fact, he had put me on his bucket list! I could not believe it. Why did he care so much to meet me? Through our messages, I told Josh that I had wrestled with my faith. I expressed the difficulty I often had being the man I wanted to be. I shared some of my specific troubles with him. He always responded to my messages with such encouragement and positivity. And now, even after his passing, Josh still had a message to share with me through his wife Annie. She grabbed my arms and looked into my eyes and said, "Do not give up.

Do not lose the faith." Two simple phrases said with genuine love.

Annie and I continued to talk about Josh. She told me how he loved me and wished he could have met me. I was able to tell her how thankful I was for the both of them coming into my life at the perfect time. We also spoke of the origin of our relationship. We both agreed that it didn't feel like we had met on the internet. In the eyes of some, we were strangers. To us, it felt as if we had known each other our entire lives. I knew that Josh's love had brought us together.

The drive home from the memorial service was intense. I was flooded with thoughts and emotions. I spent the drive thinking about Josh and his effect on me. I found myself hurting for his wife and his sister, yet also inspired by their strength. The drive was a long one, and I was forced to pull over at times when the emotions took over. It was so much to process.

As my trip continued, I thought of things I should have said. At one point, I knew that I needed to let her know something. I needed to tell her one more thing before giving her the space she needed to grieve. But I knew that I needed to wait. Annie was possibly feeling overwhelmed by all of the encouragement being poured over her in those days after Josh's death and memorial. I wanted to save my words for a later day, after the rawness had worn off. I wanted to share them at a time when her wounds were still fresh, while others had seemingly moved on.

I knew I needed to go home and process everything that had happened. I would write down some thoughts, and present them to her when the time was right. About a week later, I wrote to Annie. My desire was simply to remind her how wonderful she was, and how thankful I was for her and for Josh. My letter went something like this:

Hello. It's your dear friend Cooper. I just wanted to take the time to write you a personal letter, because...well...who doesn't love a good ol' handwritten letter? It's so hard for me to believe that it has been one week since Josh's memorial. I'm sure that for you the concept of time just feels like one big blur. Annie, I am so sorry. I wish that I could take away your pain. I wish that I could heal your heart.

Like I said at the memorial, sometimes it's so hard for me to believe that I met you and Josh on the internet. It truly feels like we have all been lifelong friends. I mean that. I really do. I am thankful for the both of you for being a part of my life. I can without a doubt say that you have both been huge blessings to me. I can't say it enough, thank you! Speaking of time!!! No joke. I had this thought on my drive home from Cincinnati. I really do hope that it brings your heart some comfort. So you know how the idea of time is supposedly different for us than it is for God? Like a million years on earth is like a day in Heaven? or something like that...? Anyhow...if this thought process is true, then picture this. While the wait for you to see Josh again might feel like an eternity, the wait for Josh to see you again, well...it will feel like seconds. Almost like...he blinked his eyes and then there you were. His beautiful Annie Belle. Annie, I know that this does not change the fact that this is extremely difficult, I know that it does not make it easy, but...I genuinely and sincerely hope that it brings your heart some joy to think of how "moments" from now, Josh will once again see the most beautiful earthly face that his eyes ever made contact with. And then…my dear, sweet friend Annie…the two of you will join together, alongside the sea of faces that will bask in the glory of our God and Savior.

Annie…I want to say it again because I mean it. I am so sorry. I am sorry. I am sorry. I am sorry. I will continue to pray for you. I will pray that each and every day the Lord will provide you with strength that you need. I will pray that you will recognize that strength. I will pray that you will then continue to allow that strength to continue to develop you into an even more amazing woman of God. I love you my dear friend. —Cooper.

-CONCLUSION-

There is a saying that all good things come to an end, but I would rather think of this as a new beginning. I spent thirty-three weeks traveling 22,000 miles, stopping in thirty-three different cities and visiting over one hundred different coffee shops. As I reflect, a sea of faces flashes through my mind.

Nine months after ending my journey, I find myself sitting in a country home, amidst the woods of central Missouri, writing this conclusion. I am attempting to constructively process all that happened during Coffee with Cooper. The nomadic season, which I thought was about me changing other people, had completely changed me. When I started, my intention was to use my story to inspire and radiate hope. I like to think that those things did, in fact, occur. But I found inspiration and hope for myself, too. I found hope in humanity. I met people who care and want to make the world better with their own lives and stories.

The day I finished my trip came earlier than planned. It was the thirty-third week of what was to be a forty-week journey. I couldn't shake the strong desire to be done.

Was I being weak? So many friends and family members were tracking my travels. Would they be disappointed in me? I was swimming in a sea of emotion and concern. Regardless, I felt as though my goal had been accomplished and I wanted to go home.

I honestly didn't know where "home" was going to be. I didn't have a place of my own. I barely had any money. I tried not to let these thoughts cloud my judgment—I needed to focus on one problem at a time. I decided to call an old friend and talk about my situation. I didn't expect him to fix anything, or even give me an answer; I just wanted to vent.

I was at a 7-Eleven in Los Angeles when I made the call. I had a Coke in my hand as the words flowed through the phone. I shared my desire to be done, but expressed an even deeper desire to just...be home. He listened, and then asked me some seemingly obvious questions. Did I really feel like anyone would be disappointed in me? Did I actually think people were going to be upset? Or would they appreciate what I had already done? Was anyone really going to consider me a failure?

My thoughts were still consumed with worry, but I found peace when I considered all of the seeds I had planted during my travels. The sowing season had occurred so sporadically, I could only hope my labors would produce a harvest. I felt confident that this was the case, simply because of the changes that had taken place in me. Surely others had been affected in the same way. I knew the last thirty-three weeks had not been lived in vain. I was not a failure.

It all became clear. I was finishing my journey early, and everything was going to be alright. I was going home.

A few days later, I packed up my belongings and prepared to head back to Missouri. The moment felt surreal. Just thirty-three weeks earlier, I had started my journey in St. Louis with my best friend, Scott. That day, the last of my Coffee with Cooper adventure, I said goodbye to Los Angeles and once again to my best friend, Scott. As I had traveled the U.S. of A, he had moved to L.A. for an internship. As if that wasn't enough irony for one day, my phone rang as I packed the car. It was a newspaper reporter from Springfield, Illinois, who had previously contacted me during the first week of my journey. He had written an article about me and my intentions, and was calling to check in on my progress. He was hoping to do a follow-up article upon my return home. There was no way he could have timed his phone call more perfectly. These two occurrences, which some may call pure coincidence, brought me the closure and peace of mind I sought only days earlier. It was like God was saying, "You're headed in exactly the right direction."

Nine months later, I still find myself reliving and attempting to process all that happened as I traveled the country. So many times I have shared stories, pictures, and memories of moments from my journey. Thoughts of those days get me through difficult days as they arise in the here and now. In the reflection of those days I find courage, assurance, hope, and faith. I find the strength to carry on when I feel tired and weak. I find confidence in my story (both the good and bad parts). And I see a better version of myself, molded by the events of those thirty-three weeks.

I am thankful for every second of my experience, and all of the people who made it possible. Thank you, to all of the hosts, the generous givers, the conversationalists, the cooks, the baristas, the silent viewers from afar, the seas of innocent bystanders, and those of you taking the time to read these words. I *thank you*. I also want to thank Annie (my editor) for spending countless hours working on making my book sound much better than I ever could have. She did this all while working full-time, maintaining a family business, being a mom to two beautiful children, and attempting to live her own life every day! She did this and she did it so perfectly! Thank you, Annie! Thank you so very much! And...I'd be a fool not to mention my second editor (that's right! I had two!). The Third set of eyes. The fresh vantage point of this project and the stories that come with it: Lynsey! Lynsey, thank you *so* much for taking your own time to invest into this dream of mine (writing a book). Without you...I truly believe it would not have been possible. Your constant encouragement has given me strength on some of my weakest days! I feel so blessed to know you and your old ball and chain Curt!

At the conclusion of what was supposed to be "*the* journey" I realize I have only completed the training for the real journey: the rest of my life. I face more days than any doctor could have ever predicted, more equipped than I could have ever imagined—here's to the next chapter!

-ABOUT THE AUTHOR-

Daniel Cooper (or Cooper as you likely know him) is an aspiring author/motivational speaker. He currently resides in Columbia, MO, at a place known as "The Farm House" with five of his closest friends. He is madly in love with his sidekick/ furry friend, Pepper Smith the Border collie.

When he is not speaking, he can easily be found drinking coffee in downtown Columbia. (A special shout-out to Kaldi's Coffee, a place he would consider his home away from home.)

Cooper tries as much as possible to be involved in the music ministry that happens at City of Hope, a church that he attends in downtown Columbia, MO. He has found a deep love and connection with many of the people that attend there.

Some of his hobbies/interests include: playing and listening to music, travel, bonfires, coffee, conversation with strangers, running, and so much more.

If you're interested in having Cooper come and share his story of cancer and/or the stories that happened on his journey, you can reach him by email at coffeewithcooper@gmail.com.

56237410R00115

Made in the USA
Charleston, SC
17 May 2016